Margaret Deitrich, Ph. D.

Secrets in the family

SECRETS
IN THE FAMILY

by LILY PINCUS
and CHRISTOPHER DARE

PANTHEON BOOKS, NEW YORK

Library of Congress Cataloging in Publication Data

Pincus, Lily.
Secrets in the Family.

Includes bibliographical references and index.
1. Family. 2. Secrecy (Psychology) 3. Inter-
personal relations. I. Dare, Christopher, joint author.
II. Title.
HQ734.P68 1978   301.42'7   77-88763
ISBN 0-394-41357-1

Manufactured in the United States of America
First American Edition

Contents

Preface

This book has grown out of our joint interest in the psychology of the family. One of us comes from a background of social work with special experience in marriage problems, the other who works in psychoanalytical and family therapy is from a background of medicine and psychiatry. Despite our difference in sex, generation and professional discipline, we have found that we have many views in common on the problems of individual development and family dynamics. We have both developed a profound interest in the unconscious network of feelings, attitudes, wishes, beliefs, longings, fears and expectations, that link family members to each other and to their past lives and past families. We share a psychodynamic approach to personal development and human relationships, and have both been influenced in important ways by the work of the Tavistock Clinic in London, where there has evolved during the half-century of its existence, an identifiable psychoanalytic frame of reference.

As well as being deeply involved in the practice of helping people in psychological distress, we both have large commitments to teaching and training. Hence this joint work is addressed to issues which we have found important to us and of interest to our students. We believe that it is of fundamental importance to many professions to have an understanding of the complexities of the relationships within families, and we are convinced that this and a readiness to get in touch with the intensity and multiplicity of feelings within the family is the essential prerequisite for intelligent and sensitive intervention in the affairs of individuals and families.

Although the data upon which we base our understanding stems from therapeutic situations, we are not addressing ourselves to the topic of treatment, whether by individual or conjoint means. Our concern is to attempt to describe aspects of the unfolding and evolving cycle of the family. We also hope that what we have written will be of interest to those who are not professionally involved with families, but eager to understand better the undercurrents of feelings and relationships in their own lives, and those of past and future generations.

Prologue. Secrets in the life cycle of the family

The most important milestones in the life cycle[1] of the family are the universal mysteries of birth, copulation and death. They have been always surrounded by social myths and taboos, and unconscious feelings connected with them have remained secret and powerful throughout human history. In the twentieth century, the psychodynamic understanding of the person has led us to realize that these unknown feelings may have harmful and inhibiting effects, and that if we can let ourselves know about our responses to these events and become aware of the experiences and feelings connected with them, then our lives need not be dominated by some of the more damaging effects of secrets and myths in the family. Secrets[2] may be private to one family-member; or tacitly shared with others; or unconsciously subscribed to by all family-members, often from generation to generation, until they become a myth.

The concept of myth[3] is not easy to define: we can use it to describe a falsification of a situation or we can use it to mean stories or legends which reveal rather than hide essential underlying truths, for instance the oedipal myth. Here it means a secret or unconscious belief or attitude which through its general acceptance by succeeding generations of a family, comes to perpetuate itself in determining their responses and behaviour. According to Ferreira, myths are to be found in practically all families, and it seems that a certain amount of family mythology may be necessary to the smooth operating of even the healthiest family relationships.

When we talk about secrets in the family, we distinguish between those that are acknowledged as actual events by a family member who keeps them secret from the others, and those which have no such factual foundation but arise from fantasies. For even without the presence of real events kept secret, feelings arising and enduring from the time when jealousy, rivalry, love and hate within the family have to be faced, may produce fantasies which, because they cannot be expressed, become secrets. Such secrets may be unconsciously shared by parents and children for generations and are sometimes not easy to distinguish from family myth. Both kinds of secret can powerfully affect the lives of individuals and whole families, and on examining them more closely it may not be easy to decide whether it is the fact or the fantasy that yields this power. There may indeed be a true fact kept secret, but it may be the fantasies attached to it that determine behaviour in the family.

Here is an example of what we would call a 'real secret'. *Mrs Abel*, an English girl from a good middle-class family, had married a wealthy man and gone to live with him in South Africa. After three years of marriage, he lost all their fortune, had a heart attack and died suddenly, leaving his wife in poverty in a strange land with two little girls aged two and one years old. Ten months after his death she had another daughter, obviously by another man, and after a year or two returned to England with her three children. Although the elder girls could later recall the occasional presence of an unexplained man, the existence of the third child's father remained unacknowledged in the family, and she grew up in an all-female household assuming that she shared a dead father with her sisters. Few memories of this dead father survived in the family, and their very loving and energetic mother apparently made up for his absence so successfully that the girls did not feel the lack of a father. The complete secrecy surrounding fathers was echoed by the exclusion of men from their family life.

When grown up, the eldest daughter married a man with an eighteen-months-old daughter by another woman and had a son by him. This man vanished mysteriously, never to be heard of again. His wife returned with both the children to her mother who made them very welcome. She continued to live with her when she had a third child, born illegitimately a few years later. Mrs Abel welcomed the role of grandmother as much as she had that of mother.

The two other daughters did not recreate so strikingly their mother's secret by having children without fathers, yet both showed a certain tendency to bring about a similar state of affairs. Although both married, their mother remained the most important person in their lives. They both handed their daughters over to her, and resumed their careers. Mrs Abel brought up her grand-daughters most lovingly, and became for them, as she had for her own children, the chief focus of their emotional development. The result was that they too grew up without developing a relationship with a father. They were never confronted with the task of learning to tolerate a three-person relationship by having to share a mother with a father, and so never worked through the conflicts of the oedipal situation. It is interesting to note how this inherited pattern was broken by one of the grand-daughters. She had a love affair with an older married man which had to be terminated when it became a danger to his marriage. In her distress she turned to her own father, whom she hardly knew, for sympathy and comfort although at this point she was unaware that the choice of her lover was an expression of her need for a father. When she now turned to him, he asked no questions but responded with love and concern, and this enabled her to free herself from the effects of the family secret.

We believe that the grandmother's conviction that women are better off without men and children without fathers, had its roots in a childhood disappointment. As a little girl she may have felt rejected and let down by her father's lack of response to her secret longings for him, longings that are universal in all little girls. These feelings were reinforced by the sudden collapse of her marriage to a man who was apparently effective, and had made her feel accepted and loved. She had welcomed being taken away from her father to the other side of the world but the loss of her husband and the failure of their life together emphasized her childhood feeling that she must not depend on men.

We heard later that the father of Mrs Abel's third baby had been—unknown to Mrs Abel—a married man with teenage children. He had offered to marry her but she learned his secret on the way to the wedding and fled. Her attraction to another father had again resulted in painful disappointment. From then on Mrs Abel put all her efforts into proving to herself, and later to her daughters and grand-daughters, that it is best to live and have children without the support of men. As she was a powerful and loving person, she largely succeeded in doing this. Her 'secret', her deep conviction that men could not be relied on, resulted in establishing a pattern of relating to men which might have turned into a myth, if it had remained unchallenged.

It is interesting that whenever a family member is able to challenge a family secret, then the attitude of other family members towards the secret also seems to change; the collusive system is broken and new facts and fantasies come into the open.

The most frequent and carefully hidden secrets are those which stem from incestuous feelings or fantasies.

Mrs Carter, then in her late thirties, asked for help because her fears of V.D. had made her own life miserable and led to friction in her family, who rebelled against her compulsive preoccupation with cleaning rituals. She thought her fears stemmed from a time when as a young woman in the army she had attended a lecture on V.D. There, she felt V.D. had been depicted as the result of sexual pleasures, and when she later married and experienced those pleasures with her husband, she was terrified that V.D. would follow, and found herself taking endless precautionary measures against it, precautions that did nothing to eliminate her fears.

In spite of Mrs Carter's distress and her urgent appeal for help, she strongly resisted attempts to get to the root of her problem, and was very reluctant to talk about her past. Slowly it emerged that she had lost her father in early infancy, but she did not miss him as her mother remarried when she was two years old, and she loved her stepfather dearly. With great pain she recalled how, when she was in her teens, this love had turned into sexual passion and how the passion was reciprocated by the stepfather. He spoiled her, took her out, gave her presents, and although her mother did not seem to notice or mind what went on, her daughter felt guilty. Joining the army was a step she took largely to get away from this situation. It meant a painful separation from the stepfather, but she tried to forget about him and repressed all memory of their physical relationship. It emerged in her therapy that the obsession about V.D., of which she had not become aware until after her marriage, was really connected with her repressed secret guilt about her sexual enjoyment with her stepfather. When she was able to recall and accept the pain connected with these denied feelings, the obsession quite dramatically disappeared.

Mrs Carter's secret was her incestuous relationship with her stepfather and the guilty feelings attached to it. The exploring of the painful secret released her and her family in a remarkable way from its damaging effects.

Whether a secret is based on a real event or on fantasies about such an event, does not seem to affect its influence.

Mr Bell was two years old when two sisters were born with one year between them. So, his mother had little time for him. When his older sister was three, he got scarlet fever and spent long miserable weeks in the isolation ward of a hospital where parents' visits were not allowed. His recollection is that when he came home he was told that his sisters had died, and he felt that he had infected and killed them, and that from this moment his parents never trusted or liked him. He responded by becoming a difficult and unhappy child, and his parents, unaware of his feelings, could not understand the great change in him.

As he grew up, he became increasingly estranged from them, joined the army at the earliest possible age and was sent abroad. He never wrote to his parents and wanted to believe that he could forget his unhappy past. After his marriage, he and his wife settled in a comfortable home and had two daughters. Mr Bell worked as a bricklayer and being an excellent worker was repeatedly offered the post of a foreman. He always refused it, as he felt unable to accept responsibility for others. When an apprentice who worked with him had a motor-cycle accident, Mr Bell had a mental breakdown and accused himself of having caused the accident. During a short stay in a mental hospital, his psychiatrist helped him to make the link between his present anxieties and those caused by his sisters' deaths and encouraged Mr Bell to make contact with his parents again. They were delighted to be reunited with him and to get to know their only grandchildren.

In talking to his father about the past, it emerged that the deaths of his sisters were in no way connected with his scarlet fever. One of them had died of meningitis a year before his illness and the other one some time after it as a result of a car accident.

Such a startling misremembering, responsible for so much unhappiness in two generations, becomes understandable if we remember the anger and jealousy that a two-year-old child has to cope with if he is supplanted, as Mr Bell was, by younger siblings. His retaliatory fantasies of eliminating the resented sisters would have been alarmingly dramatized by the death of one of them when he was four, and a year later, struggling with the traumatic experience of separation from his parents during the many weeks' stay in the isolation ward, he had to 'forget' his sister's death in order to escape his fears that he too might disappear for ever as she had. Telescoped by fever-delirium and isolation, his murderous fantasies became so strong that he completely lost touch with reality. Finally the death of his second sister—a real event coinciding so closely with his secret fantasies and fears—made it absolutely imperative for him to push these memories out of his conscious mind. His parents, perhaps because of their own sense of guilt, were evidently unable to understand his fears and explain to him what had actually happened, and he was left with nothing but a secret certainty of his own guilt and responsibility for his sisters' deaths.

When many years later a young apprentice in his care had an accident, his fantasies were vividly evoked. His mental breakdown may have been in part an unconscious attempt to pay retribution for what he felt he had done, and perhaps it was also an expression of his fear that his secret, if it remained unexplored and unchallenged, might have the power to endanger the lives of his daughters, who were now at the age when he thought his sisters had died.

Often the origin of a family myth is lost but that does not seem to undermine its power. It may be used to confirm anxiety-raising patterns which have been handed on from one generation to another. Frequently a similar myth in both partners' families may contribute to the choice of a marriage partner; thus it becomes a shared myth, springing from and continually stimulating the same shared fantasy.

At times myths constitute a blatant distortion of facts. For example, *Mr Shields* was one year old when his father returned home from the Boer War as an invalid. Whether any specific illness had been diagnosed was not clear to the son, but he knew that his father never worked again and spent the rest of his life drinking on his wife's meagre earnings and treating her violently when she complained. Mr Shields joined his mother and sisters in fearing and despising the drunken father, but with the help of photographs of the father in army uniform and a medal from the Boer War, the family cherished an image of him as a war hero. They had also been brought up to cherish the memory of their grandfather, the father's father, who they believed had been a great soldier and died young as the result of his service injuries. Much later, this turned out to be a complete invention.

By believing in these two generations of heroes, Mr Shields seemed to rescue from the destroyed image of his father something to support his own potency. From earliest childhood the boy played soldier; later he became a member of a youth club with military ambitions, and when grown up, although he worked as a clerk for his regular job, he became an enthusiastic member of the Territorials. When the Second World War broke out, he was called up and sent on a course to learn to drive army lorries, and seems, from the recollections of his children, to have needed to tell dramatic stories about their size and power. When he was due to go to the front, he developed a paralysis of his right leg, which earned him a discharge from the army with a service medal and a disability pension. The army doctors diagnosed the paralysis as psychosomatic, assuming the cause to be terror of getting involved in action. Mr Shields denied this with passion, and for the rest of his life complained of severe bouts of pain and remained a semi-invalid. Frequent subsequent medical investigations revealed nothing that could explain the pains of his disability but he was able to persuade his family to believe that a major operation which might have offered some hope for a cure was too risky in view of his general medical condition. Nevertheless he insisted that he had had some surgery and liked showing off to family and friends a piece of bone removed from his spine.

His wife had her own reasons for maintaining the myth that her husband was a powerful if disabled man. She had had an older sister who had died at the age of four, a year before she herself was born. The photos of this lovely fair-haired girl, and her mother's frequent stories of how inconsolable her father had been at the loss of this enchanting child, impressed on her what a disappointment she herself was for her parents. She was caught in the all-too-common myth of those who have a dead brother or sister, that the ideal best-loved child has died, and the surviving one is inferior—a myth that cannot be challenged by the reality of a growing child. When this woman met her husband, he appeared to be a big powerful man in his Territorial Army uniform. In marrying him she hoped to gain value in her parents' eyes as well as in her own. Later, in the face of his weakness and collapse, she was driven to collude with him in the myth that his disablement was the cause for his failure to reach his full potential. Although his sons suffered from their pompous attention-seeking father, they too colluded unquestioningly in support of the myth. Nevertheless the father's conviction that the sons had inherited his frustrated power gave them some confidence in their own ability. The eldest son particularly had a strong drive to be, as it were, the 'Crown Prince' who would fulfil the sick king's thwarted ambition. He became a successful potent man, strong enough to choose an independent self-assured wife. At a time when he made a great step forward in his career and status, the father who was now in his seventies, showed signs of considerable deterioration. It seemed he could no longer maintain his life of lies; his behaviour became increasingly bizarre, and his wife felt that she could no longer tolerate life with him. His G.P. began to think of a mental hospital stay when the son, fortified perhaps by his own recent real success in a competitive world as well as by the conviction that it was the only alternative to a complete mental breakdown, decided to try to challenge his father and the family myth—by revealing to him his knowledge (accidentally gained) that the story of the spinal operation was a lie, and the piece of bone simply a fragment he had picked up somewhere. The father's immediate response was furious denial, but his son's insistence on the need to face the truth, coupled with his genuine concern for his father's welfare, enabled the latter to calm down.

It is clear that for Mr Shields, as for his father and grandfather, the myth of their power was necessary to support the false versions of themselves which were all they could afford to acknowledge. By the time a man has relied for a lifetime on such self-deception it is difficult even to wish to change, still more to achieve sufficient change in the self to manage life without the support of his myths; especially as long as members of the family need to maintain secrets and myths for reasons of their own.

When it became clear to Mr Shields that his son could challenge the family myth because he was secure enough in his strength and his true self, he, the father, too was able to relax his grip on the myth and subsequently became able to behave more rationally.

Secrets and myths may, as we have seen in these stories, be started by an individual member of the family. Like everything else that happens in families, they do not remain the property of the individual, as the responses of other family members set in motion processes of interaction, which strengthen or weaken the effects of secrets and myths.

Fundamentally they are always about power and dependence, about love and hate, about the wish to take care of and the wish to hurt, feelings which are inevitably bound up with sex, birth and death. At the time when the child has a first awareness of having to cope with this mixture of powerful and often contradicting feelings, secret wishes and longings begin to dominate his private world. We shall try to show how this private world remains throughout our lives a source of pain and conflicts but also the source of our imagination and our creativity.

1. The development of the person

The main purpose of this book is to show our way of understanding how families grow and develop. Each member of the family continues to change and, hopefully, grows emotionally even when physical growth is complete. Each stage of the life of the individual family members contains conflicts between the urges that come from the inner wishes and longings of the person and the opposing pressure to conform to the needs of the outside world of people and things. Our love and longings for closeness and for a return of love from other people mean that we attempt to suppress some of our most selfish but intense wishes. That suppression usually succeeds in restraining purely self-centred activities and even curtails our awareness of some of these wishes. However, the inner urges and wishes remain, and constitute the 'secret' mental life of the individual. The shared and unshared inner wishes of the different family members are the sources of the family secrets that we refer to in our title and of which we tried to give examples in our first chapter.

This present chapter, which is more theoretical than most of the book, is an account of the development of the individual.[4] It is provided at this point for reference and may either be read straight through or referred to section by section in conjunction with the subsequent chapters. Each of the subsequent chapters are devoted to the effects on the family life cycle of specific stages of individual development. We concentrate on those stages of development that make for what we may call 'crisis' in the life of the individual. Because of the influence of family relationships, a crisis for an individual in the family makes for a critical time for the family as a whole.

This relationship between individual and family crises is underlined in our discussion of the stages of the development of the family. We describe here how the infant, child and young person, as he grows and changes, experiences both the self and the outside world and, from the beginning, makes his own unique personality by attempting to integrate inner needs with the realities and demands of the outside world.

D. W. Winnicott has well described this balance of the inner life of the individual and the family environment in which development takes place: 'Each individual child by healthy emotional growth and by the development of his or her personality in a satisfactory way, promotes the family and the family atmosphere. The parents, in their efforts to build a family, benefit from the sum of the integrative tendencies of the individual children.'[5]

We will try to emphasize, over and over again, that we believe that tensions and conflicts are necessary to continuing growth, which comes about by finding ways of integrating the different aspects of the self in response to the changing demands of development.

In the following sections we describe the tasks of each stage of development, concentrating upon the demands that we see as being paramount in the person's subjective experience of himself. In each we stress those aspects of development that have a particular quality of presenting a demand for response and adaptation by the other members of the family. It is also worth re-asserting that each phase is never completely lost or totally forgotten. There can never be a fulfilment of the needs of one phase so complete that the person never experiences similar feelings again. On the contrary, we see each phase as leaving indelible imprints not only on the way the individual approaches the next stage, but also upon the whole pattern of his future needs. As we point out in the chapter on marriage, needs from all previous phases of life, as well as those strictly appropriate to adulthood, will be present in the grown-up members of the family.

THE PSYCHOLOGY OF THE BABY

In our professional work we, the authors, are principally concerned with the subjective experiences of people struggling to achieve happiness or, at least, trying to get some freedom from their repetitive patterns of distress and pain. We always try to understand how configurations of feelings and actions in the present come out of past patterns of experience. We think that we can frequently make out patterns that come from the early life of the person, even back to infancy. We realize, however, the great difficulties in talking of the psychology of little children who are unable to tell us in speech of their feelings, wishes, attitudes and beliefs. We have to rely, in part, on our empathic understanding and also on attempts to recreate in our own minds, and in the minds of our patients and clients, what it might be like to be a baby. Freud, A. Freud, M. Klein, Winnicott and Balint[6] have illuminated different aspects of the possible mental life of the baby. Their conclusions do not always agree, especially with regard to the first few weeks of life, but what we write here is a consensus of psychoanalytic views as we interpret them in the light of our own personal and professional experience.

It is quite clear that, because of the physical weakness and helplessness of the human newborn infant, survival is impossible without dedicated mothering (which can be given by a man or a woman). To the outside observer, therefore, it is clear that the psychological as well as the biological survival of the infant is dependent on an immense amount of care. We do not know at what stage the baby itself becomes aware of this state of affairs. We assume that it takes some time for the baby to achieve this awareness. What we do know is that within a few weeks of birth the baby becomes especially *aware* of the chief caring person (the mother). This is shown by the particular alertness and activity of the baby when the mother's face is visible or her voice is audible. We also know that the little baby uses its mouth to recognize, enjoy and to explore the world, especially the portion of the world that is mother. Erikson[7] says: 'As the newborn infant is separated from his symbiosis with the mother's body, his inborn and more or less co-ordinated ability to take in by mouth meets the mother's more or less co-ordinated ability and intention to feed and welcome him. At this point he lives through, and loves with, his mouth; and the mother lives through, and loves with, her breasts.' The ability of the mother to meet the baby's needs accurately and quickly has been seen by all psychoanalysts as likely to be a major influence on the baby's dawning experience of itself. Freud[8] (1923), stressed the view that the little infant had no capacity to *know* that the outside world existed or supported the baby's life. Fairbairn[9] (1952), Klein[10] (1957) and Balint[11] (1968), believed that right from the start, the baby has some experiences of aspects of the mother as occurring outside the baby's self. We are sure, as we have said, that the baby pays close attention to the mother very soon, and earliest emotional life is concentrated on that relationship. However any knowledge or feeling the baby may have that there is a caring mother to protect him, is fragile and easily overthrown by discomfort. Very rapidly, any discomfort can precipitate the baby into anger and despair that soon verges upon panic. 'Good-enough care' brings joyful bliss. The well-being of the baby requires that the mothering-person should be capable of experiencing the baby's needs almost as though those needs were the mother's own. At the time that the baby goes into a panic, we believe that his experience is like terror, disintegration or fear of annihilation. Gentle, firm loving and holding of the baby provides experiences which, in the end, can be used by the baby to manage such panic states. The value of holding for the baby is one reason for our life-long need for cuddling.

The baby's dreams may serve for the time being to satisfy his needs in so far as these are not being met by the mother. These dreams are thought of as hallucinatory gratification of wishes. As the intensity of the needs underlying the wish increases and reaches the point of discomfort, the baby becomes uncomfortable and upset and has a further technique for attempting the elimination of discomfort. This technique is the development of the belief, at least momentarily, that the discomfort does not belong to the child but is somewhere outside of the self. This process is the basis of the mechanisms of projection which are used throughout life to cope with painful or unacceptable experiences.

In our chapter on marriage we are pointing out that we think that the process of projection is central to the nature of human relationships. Here we want to trace the origins of the tendency both to believe that our wishes are being granted, and to cope with the discomfort of unfulfilled needs by projection, back to the earliest mental processes of the baby. It is the work of later stages of development, to discover ways of continuing to be able to have dreams and illusions while at the same time forming them into realistic plans and wishes. We must also learn to allow ourselves to use projections as a part of our coping skills which serve to enrich our relationships. As we will be showing in the chapter on making room for the baby, the nature of a new baby's individual qualities, as well as the general problems of the changes in family life that a baby requires, will create a developmental crisis, and hence an important growth point, for the family as an entity. No person ever completely loses the needs that were first experienced in the mother-infant relationship. They persist, and patterns of relationships which had their origins in babyhood are repeated. Therefore, we can discover, sometimes, in the relationships of children and adults, evidence of infancy experiences. This is especially so in the marital relationship, in the response of adults to babies in their care, and in certain intense therapeutic relationships. It is from these investigations that many psychoanalytical understandings of babyhood are derived.

THE BABY BECOMES A PERSON

We follow Winnicott[12] in believing that: '. . . at certain moments and over certain periods and in certain relationships, the infant of one year is a whole person.' Through the mothering person's dedication and adoration, the baby survives and soon begins to have a personality. The mother, by accepting the baby's angry and destructive feelings without retaliation, helps the baby begin the lifelong task of being able to contain and to be responsible for the capacity to hate and hurt. The mother's (and father's) adoration helps the baby begin to become someone who has sufficiently good self-appreciation and self-confidence to be able to love others. The caring persons' capacity to allow the baby's needs to override their own, helps the baby to become a person capable of caring for others. The fact that the young child's needs are met more or less accurately and more or less in time helps the baby to become trusting and reasonably optimistic. If these aspects of mothering are deficient, then the infant will attempt to look to its own needs. This is the stimulus for the development of a premature self-caring that Winnicott calls the 'False-Self'.[13] If on the other hand the baby does not experience *some* frustration of needs, then the realization of a sense of self is likely to be delayed and distorted. By the end of the first year the baby is very well aware that the mother is a separate person and has some appreciation that she too has needs for caring and protection.

At this time too—as the child begins to be able to move effectively, some safety sense and self-protection must develop. The child is becoming a separate person, who knows of the capacity to hate and hurt the people who are also loved and cared for.

As the second year is entered upon and the child is increasingly mobile, the realization of the capacity for separation from the mother causes many children to go through a clinging phase. Moreover the child can find pleasure in hurting and controlling. Such feelings may, in the child's mind, be enormously exaggerated, ('omnipotence'). His fears are aroused by his own apparently ungovernable impulses but at the same time he hopes that the power to control the mother will be sufficient to stop her desertion in the face of his own cruelty and demandingness. These crises of cruelty and independence will be shown to put the family of the little child into a crisis as well. For the baby is not now a helpless little infant, but a more separate person with individual qualities that have to be respected.

Freud considered that this crisis has its origins in the child's sensual life, and that the emotional struggle with the mother is centred on the sensually dominant zone of the child, (namely the anus), and on the control of the baby's bowels (hence the term the 'anal phase'). We think that the toddler's interests in mess and his indifference to shame constitute a stress for the family, as do the wishes for sadistic pleasures, his controlling omnipotence and his strivings to reconcile his contradictory needs for closeness and separateness. We think that we see reflections of this phase in certain sorts of marital relationships. For example those in which each partner feels a repetitive need to give and to receive cruelty and hurt, (sado-masochistic relationships), seem to contain outcomes of toddler experiences. Marriage in which there are struggles over control combined with dependent clinging, may also come about when both parents had painful experiences in the toddler time of their lives. Crises of love between husband and wife, daughter or son, mother and father, around becoming separate and declaring independence, are likely to arouse feelings from toddler times, when these issues were first embattled.

The child in the second year begins to be clearly a boy or a girl psychologically and begins to notice the biological differences between the two sexes of the children and adults of the family. The play, activity level and choice of toys show how the child is becoming aligned to masculinity or femininity. The parents and older children that the child now copies will be chosen for identification by gender as well as by love. Whether or not these gender differences are nothing but culturally determined stereotypes and ought, as some people strenuously maintain, to be discouraged, clearly little boys now begin to identify themselves with their father, want to wear his shoes, or hats, see themselves as workmen or engineers; love cars, trains and construction vehicles. Little girls copy their mother in housework and love of clothes, play with dolls and show that they see them as baby-like objects.

Freud traced some of the envy that women feel of men to elements of the little girl's admiration for and envy of the boy's penis. Karen Horney[14] was the first to point out that the little boy envies the fact that the girl becomes capable of having a baby, whilst Klein[15] saw that at some stage all children are envious of the mother's feeding resources and this is shown by a man's mixed feelings about a woman's breasts—loving them and admiring them, but disparaging them by the words used to describe them. These very early realizations of physical bodily sexual differences and the parental responses to the child's curiosity about and pleasure in, their own and others genital organs, will begin to shape the growing toddlers' dawning sexual interests. A girl who feels that little boys have a better time in life, and who admires the masculine role may either try to emulate males, or may, by reaction, despise them. The father's love and admiration for her can counteract such tendencies. The love of, and for, her mother, if the mother has found fulfilment, joy and contentment in her sex, will also further the process.

Little boys are likely to admire and envy their mother's creativity. If the envy is too strong it can make the growing boy deny longings for a woman's love. To be safe and confident in becoming a man he needs his mother's admiration of his boyish activity and liveliness to enable him to be pleased to be a boy. His love for, and identification with his father, and his realization that his mother admires and loves her husband, also reconcile him to his own inability to have babies.

We consider, therefore, that the three- to four-year-old child, who has managed to cope with some of these independence/dependence and male/female issues will have done a lot of important work towards becoming a secure person, with a confidence and pleasure in the general tendencies of his life. Such a child will already have experienced, as we have noted, a long life of dreams, fantasies, wishes and conflicts. A life of secret expectations and beliefs will have gone on alongside the development of his increasingly socialized self. These secrets will continue to influence the child in subsequent relationships.

But the next stage of development is the one that we believe creates the most important secrets influential in the formation of marital patterns and the structures of the family. This is the famous oedipus stage. This situation comes about for two reasons. Firstly, the child slowly becomes capable of really engaging in relationships with two people at a time. Clearly, very little children show that there is room in their hearts for several loves. The infant and toddler who so loves and needs mother, will none the less show great pleasure and strivings towards father, grandparents and sibs, when sufficient frequency of contact occurs. Observation does not suggest that such a situation arouses much psychological conflict for the little child. A one or two year old may show some hesitations on being faced with two loved persons offering enticing laps or embraces but there is unlikely to be any enduring conflict. Similarly a young toddler may show a wish to get rid of a rival adult or child interposed between him and his mother. There is no evidence that this generally produces a lasting mental conflict for the toddler. His problem appears to be one of divided attraction and dog in the manger possessiveness. This early stage was named by Rickman[16] and later Balint,[17] as the two person stage of object-relations. There comes a time when the child experiences the situation differently: he loves both parents, but feels the tug of conflicting love, loyalty and rivalry. Problems of jealousy and sharing come when the child, knowing that he or she loves mother, knows also that he or she loves father, and can also realize that mother and father have a special love for each other. *It is the awareness that the two people with whom the child is involved, have themselves an involvement with each other from which the child will actually, in fear or fantasy, be excluded, that constitutes the essence of the oedipal situation as a three person situation.* This is the first aspect of the oedipal complex as a stage of development.

The second crucial aspect of the oedipus complex is that it involves intense and simultaneously experienced emotions of loving and hating. The little boy knows that he loves mother. He knows he experiences his love as an intense, possessive passion, which he also begins to associate with sensations in his penis that he enjoys. He vaguely believes them to be linked to some of the reasons why his parents sleep together. This newly sensed sexual aspect of the boy's love of mother turns his father into a rival. The little boy still under the grip of the cruel, retaliatory style of thought of his earlier years, fears that his father would treat him as a dangerous rival (which the strength of his passionate need for his mother makes him to be). He may also realize that he is in fact loved by his mother, with an intensity and admiration which really do cause his father some pangs of jealousy and resentment. The problem is, that at the same time as hating and fearing his father, the little boy loves, admires and devotes himself to his father. In so far as he has modelled some of himself on his mother, he may even entertain thoughts of being a partner for his father's love, as is his mother. Moreover, the father experiences love of his little son, and cannot but be moved by his soft, straight little body.

The little boy is pulled both ways. His loves give rise to a complex, conflicting mixture of love, hate, rivalry, jealousy and puzzlement. At all stages, the child's love of and consequent intense identification with his parents makes him both want to be like each parent and also complementary to each.

The situation of the little girl has many similarities. Both are learning to add a new relationship to their established love of mother. But where the boy has to add on a relationship to a like-sex person, father, the girl's love for mother is complemented by her heterosexual love. She loves and adores her father and has some inkling of wanting to consummate that love in her physical contact with him. She has sensed his arousal and desire for her mother, and may also have had some evidence that he has had such feelings for her, albeit they have been unexpressed in any overt way. Most little girls of four to five have quite consciously wanted to marry their father, although they may have little conscious knowledge of what the exact nature of their physical relationship might be and how it might relate to their own stimulation of their genitals.

The little girl still of course has her intense, needful and loving attachment to her mother and probably has an active physical loving contact with her, which she does not want to lose. Again, like the boy she may have fantasies of being a partner to her mother as is her father. The little girl fears mother's vengeful rivalry, for she has designs on her husband. It is the sexual jealousy, rivalry and fear of retaliation that was first emphasized as the essence of the oedipal complex.

Freud[18] believed that the strength of the conscience (the super-ego) of the socialized adult, is the outcome of the child's struggle in managing the oedipal situation. He suggested that its inevitable disappointments cause the child's sexuality to be suppressed during the next few years of life.

We feel that it is extremely important that the child's love of the parent in the oedipal situation is met, in close and growing families, by the parents' love for the child. The so-called positive oedipus complex, the love of the child for the opposite-sex parent, (and the concomitant fear of the jealousy, rivalry and vengefulness of the like-sex parent that goes with this), is usually tacitly encouraged by the parents. We think that the 'normal' parent enjoys having a love relationship with his or her young, eager offspring.

For this reason the incestuous dangers of the situation are necessarily never far below the surface. The child who is in absolutely no danger of its parent of the opposite-sex having incestuous feelings towards him is more likely to become a somewhat rejected, unsure person, lacking in the hope of becoming lovable and desirable, rather than secure and confident. The fact that in usual circumstances the incestuous possibilities are highly unacceptable, consciously and socially, and indeed if enacted would endanger the child, accounts for the intensity of feeling attached to secrets arising from the oedipus situation. We believe that this intensity also accounts for their pervasiveness in the underlying psychology of family life.

THE BEGINNINGS OF THE NEW ADULT

The next period of child development, which covers in our culture the first five years of schooling, is marked by great changes in the child's knowledge, competence, skills, confidence and ability to relate to an increasing range of friends, almost exclusively of the same sex, relatives and adults. Our view is that this development comes from the child's success in coming to terms with the tasks imposed by the pre-oedipal and oedipal years. The acceptance of the inevitability of the parents' love for each other and of the double set of feelings the child has for each parent, (which implies acceptance of the contradicting experience of the oedipus complex), means that the child is able to move confidently into the school. The confidence and security gained in surviving the triangular relationship with the parents and those the child has for his sibs, makes the child ready to use skills and ability in the school situation. Teachers of both sexes can be related to, and are comfortable sources of information and knowledge. Peer culture becomes increasingly important, absorbing and identity confirming. Much of this can be disturbed by unresolved problems of the preceding stages, and family problems may appear if the child's departure to school re-arouses separation conflicts in the parents. These too are especially potent as repetitions of conflicts from preceding phases of the child's life.

It is with the stirrings of sexual maturations in pre-adolescence that the next major tasks of psychological development arise and also set up fresh tasks in family growth. The impending physical maturity of the child seems to us to be of especial importance for the family as it foreshadows the arrival of a new adult in the family group.

For the child beginning to find his or her body changing as well as undergoing a spurt of growth, pre-adolescence is a puzzling time. The body changes *shape*; bosoms appear; hair grows in previously smooth areas; the hands and feet are further away from the body. It takes time to grow accustomed to the new larger body. The 'gangling' youth is unusually clumsy and graceless in his movements. Self-consciousness about voice changes in the boy, and about normal shapeliness in girls, is accompanied by varying mixtures of pride and shame. Facial hair causes most boys pride, but feelings about genital hair are more complicated. The child begins to see his or her own genitals as resembling his or her observations of adults. Even more important, of course, is the fact that the obvious physical changes in the body, are accompanied by unseen hormonal changes, controlling growth and maturation, but also making the child *feel* different. Sexual arousal both as an awareness of wishes and as a knowledge of physical sensation in genitals and breasts, forces the child to face its sexuality. This is exciting, bewildering, frustrating and frightening and causes hesitations as well as exuberance.

At that time the world begins to require the young person to be more adult. The child, bewildered by the rapid change within, finds that new external demands are made. It is no wonder that pre-adolescence is a trying time, as so much preparatory psychological work has to go on. It is no wonder, either, that the family responds to the stress, as well. For the family, the young girl's first menstrual period is especially important as signifying the impending womanhood of the daughter. The boy's first seminal emission is not, of course, a family event in the same way. However, it signifies the evidence of the new adult coming into being in the midst of the family.

ADOLESCENCE

During adolescence the child-orientated institution of school must be left and adult-orientated work, vocational training or higher education is undertaken. The sexuality of adolescents is acknowledged legally as they reach the age of consent: two years later they receive the right to vote and to serve as jurors. The state may require that they undertake military service, if national needs demand it, and, if in gainful employment, the state demands contributions to tax, national insurance and pension payments. All these indicate that the person who until recently has been seen by the outside world and the self as a child is now being regarded as an adult. Earlier psychological work will have enabled the person, by the review and reworking of childhood experiences, to have a perspective of himself as becoming grown up. We emphasize that that process usually is accompanied by episodes of unhappiness, uncertainty and, as part of normality, some outward signs of the distress and the pain of change. Similarly, we see later adolescence as likely to be associated with episodes of personal discomfort, puzzlement, discouragement and withdrawal. These inner distresses may present themselves as periods of depression, awkward behaviour, unsociability and unpredictability. The symptoms appear less frequently in the later than in the earlier stages of adolescence, but disturbance in later adolescence, if it does occur, is more likely to show itself as serious delinquency or mental breakdown.

We find that one of the most useful ways of understanding the inner psychological processes of later adolescence is to consider the period in terms of Erikson's[19] 'identity crisis'. Erikson says: 'It (the identity crisis) occurs in that period of the life cycle when each youth must forge for himself some central perspective and direction, some working unity, out of the effective remnants of his childhood and the hope of his anticipated adulthood; he must detect some meaningful resemblance between what he has come to see in himself and what his sharpened awareness tells him others judge and expect him to be.' It is as if the youth has come to the stage when all the multitudinous possibilities for personal style and self-expression can be tried out in adult freedom, but in expectation, too, of adult responsibilities. In later adolescence, most people begin to experiment with *actual* relationships in attempts to fulfil their previously largely fantasised inner longings. The freedom of adulthood allows the person to engage in a number of relationships. They all contain elements of a wish to establish a certain pattern. Some relationships will do so *in part*. The adolescent begins to learn which of the aspects of personal wishes can be expected to meet actual gratifications. This is a testing out of the wishes and the possibilities of the self. Experiment in relationship, and this includes experiment with the physical possibilities of the sexual self, helps the adolescent to realize which wishes he wants to represent in his actual life and which do not need, necessarily, to be put into practice. Heightened awareness of the priorities of the inner needs gained by actual experiences enables the individual to attempt fresh relationships which gradually move him towards more persistent and stable relationships.

The implications of the experiments and changes of adolescence and the extent to which these processes take the adolescent along the family path or away from it, will have great importance for the development of the family. There is a continuity of development of the personality through infancy and childhood to late adolescence. Previous experiences can be tried out in partial re-enactments and recreations as the adolescent finds his own style and consistency. Blos says: 'Infantile conflicts are not removed at the close of adolescence, but they are rendered specific, they become ego-syntonic, i.e. they become integrated within the realm of the ego as life tasks. They become centred within the adult self representations.' We are impressed by the extent to which oedipal aspects of the conflicts of infancy determine adolescent and adult love choices.

Across the whole area of psychological choice, in life style, attitudes, preferred role in relationships, leisure activity, political and religious affiliations, and so on, the adolescent tries to find a match between his own self and the repertoire available in the real world. The actual range of choice depends on what society makes available to the individual, within his background, at that time. But the particular mixture of styles a person finds himself adopting is his attempt to fulfil his needs for personality growth and self-enhancement. A job, a profession, a faith will be chosen partly because it is available but also because it fits the person's needs. In later adolescence, as in the remainder of life, relationships are entered into in order to give a sense of completion and fulfilment of the self. Such completion comes about from perceiving the partner one loves in a relationship need pattern. But when a relationship expresses the love needs of both partners, there are still other needs and experiences from previous family life, which are not expressed in that love relationship. For both partners a baby, born of the partnership, will have a meaning and significance derived from their unfulfilled childhood longings, persisting through adolescence. Parenthood is enjoyed as a part of the completion of personal growth and development.

2. The secret contract of marriage

In this chapter we will be trying to do two things. Firstly, we shall say something about marriage, or at least about how we understand the psychology of marriage. Secondly, we will be trying to introduce a general approach to understanding how people function, and in particular how they relate to each other. This is indeed the main theme of the book throughout.[20]

To illustrate our way of thinking, we will give descriptions of families whom we got to know professionally because they found themselves in difficulties. The marriages which we describe here may therefore give the impression that we have a pessimistic view of human relationships that tends to emphasize the confusions and frustrations, and stresses about what can go wrong in the course of a marriage. We hope to show, however, that despite our daily experience of the vulnerability of marriage, we do not take a gloomy view of this institution in spite of our awareness of the changes going on in society and in social attitudes which apparently threaten the long term survival of marriage in its current form. We think that the problems that bring people to us to talk of the difficulties they are having in their marriages, or with the events in the lives of their children, do not mark our clients and patients off as a group of people who run their lives in a very different way from the majority of us. Marriages vary greatly not only in the degree of satisfaction the couples obtain but also in the sort of satisfaction they seek. The stability they can achieve in their marriage is paradoxically dependent upon the flexibility with which each can respond to his or her own and the partner's changing needs. The difference between so-called 'satisfactory' and 'unsatisfactory' marriages, as well as between those couples who seek help and those who do not, is not a fundamental difference of kind but one of degree. We think that all marriages, like all other human relationships, have aspects of satisfaction and aspects of conflict, a feature which is implicit in the human condition. It is because of the potential which marriage offers for the development of the personality, and hopefully for the healing of old wounds that we consider it to be such a valuable institution. There is no marriage without conflict, and coming to terms with conflict makes for growth and development. For most people the conscious decision to marry is an attempt to find happiness and comfort rather than to solve conflicts. Yet at some level of their minds most couples know that the latter is inseparable from the former.

We base our study of marriage on certain general principles[21] which are ways of looking at relationships. The first principle that seems of great importance to us is that the motivations that take people into marriage, sustain its perpetuation and give it its particular qualities, are largely unconscious. In using the word *unconscious* we are following Freud's[22] view that it can have a twofold meaning. Firstly something that is apparently unconscious may be so, simply because the person cannot or need not, for the moment, bring the thought to mind. Secondly the thought, motive, wish or fantasy of which the person is unconscious may be forcibly kept out of consciousness so that its existence can only be surmised indirectly. Motivations for marriage are unconscious in the second sense and this implies that it is rarely possible to gain, by direct questioning, any cogent reasons from someone about his choice of spouse or the nature of the marriage. If we ask anyone why he married a particular person and why the marriage works the way it does, we are likely to be given a few mild generalities, which are hardly convincing reasons for the endurance of the partnership. For example, one pair of pensioners when asked what had sustained their marriage over forty years, said that their marriage had worked because each was determined to have at least one friend who they would not share with the other one. When asked why they had chosen each other, the wife said that she had admired her husband for standing up against petty regulations at work: 'I could see he was a man of principle'. The husband could not easily put into words what had at first made him think that he could marry the girl who became his wife but then said: 'You know, she reminded me of Greta Garbo, without it seeming at all that she wanted to look like her.' It is quite likely that these sparse comments covered a number of very important reasons for their marriage, but they did not know why these things should be so important to them, or how they fitted into their lives and personalities. It seems to us to be obvious that the reasons for the suddenness and intensity of falling in love are usually unconscious. The choice of a marriage partner seems often to have been made very quickly, on the basis of relatively little conscious knowledge, and with, as it turns out, great accuracy of complementarity and fit of personalities and even life experience of the partners. Couples quite often turn out to have had striking similarities in aspects of childhood experiences, which they only discover after they have married or made a decision to marry. To quote Dr Henry Dicks: 'None of us know by what sixth sense persons of the opposite sex recognize each other as suitable for working out their complex and often internally contradictory need systems.'

An important aspect of unconscious mental functioning is that the person tends to cope with unfulfilled wishes and with painful feelings by a variety of self-protective devices, (the 'defence mechanisms' described by A. Freud).[23] One of the ways those mechanisms work is that when painful feelings or longed-for wishes are pushed out of the mind, they are repressed. But perhaps the most common techniques for coping with intense wishes that cannot be granted are to daydream about them, accepting a delay in their fulfilment, and finding a partial and often symbolic substitute.

In our view most unfulfilled wishes involve another person, and many painful feelings are also connected with thoughts about, and responses to, someone else. Wishes and pains that are related in fantasy to longings about another person, may affect our relationships in real life as well as on a fantasy level. We may try to put our feelings outside us, a process generally called projection. (Also discussed in Chapter 1.)

This mechanism of projection, through which feelings and ideas from inside a person are attributed to people and objects outside, is in itself a normal part of all relationships. We do not know how people manage to put feelings (which may be either appropriate or inappropriate to the situation in which they find themselves), out of their own psychological system into that of another person. We do know, however, from direct observation, that people can do this, and unknowingly have to do so when the feelings are too painful or too highly charged for them to be able to hold on to them in their own minds.

Such processes of projection go on in all relationships but are especially powerful in those that embody the strongest emotional ties. Marriage, therefore, offers them a particularly fruitful field; indeed projection processes may well have been involved in the original choice of a partner who is able and willing to accept and act out, at least in part, some of what the other one needs to project.

Such choices can have profound therapeutic features, if each partner is able to make contact in the other with those aspects of himself which he has not developed. As R. D. Laing[24] puts it: 'Each partner strives to find in the other, or induces the other to become, the very embodiment of the other whose co-operation is required as a complement of the particular identity he feels compelled to sustain.'

Whether or not there can be mutual gratification, growth and maturation turns in large measure on how much of the personality is got rid of in this way; the degree of violence with which the mental act is carried out, and the rigidity with which it is maintained. How often have we heard a husband say proudly: 'My wife always gets her way. She ticks people off right and proper'. And one feels that he wants her to do this partly *for him* because he cannot do it directly; or the wife may say: 'I get so irritable with the children but my husband never loses his temper. I can always be sure of his patience, and it doesn't matter so much if I am a bit hasty.' She attributes all the patience in the family to him, relying on him to prevent things from getting out of control. We can see that the use of projection in marriages and families is not just an attempt to get rid of unwanted feelings or aspects of the self. If such feelings and parts of the self are projected onto a family member, they are not lost. Moreover, because they are now experienced as part of a loved person, they may lose some of the anxiety they used to produce, and in time may even appear sufficiently acceptable to be taken back into the self. In other words, the loved person may make it possible to remain in touch with some aspects of the self that can be accepted in a married partner but cannot be expressed directly by the self. The same process can often be seen to operate in a parent-child relationship, where the child can express for the parent feelings that the parents could not tolerate in himself. (See Chapter 5.)

However, when one partner forces on to the other aspects of himself which are very frightening to him, such as depression or aggression, even though he needs the partner to express them for him, he may condemn and attack him or her for doing just that. The same dynamics which led to the original choice in the hope of resolving anxieties, may then trap the couple into a vicious circle;

the partner who has projected the frightening aspects of himself into the other, may dissociate himself more and more from them, thus forcing the other to express them all in a double dose. The result is increasing anxiety for both.

We will illustrate this by an example: A quiet passive man who hated unpleasantness asked for help because his wife was so aggressive towards his mother, with whom the couple lived and who had always been ill with heart disease. The husband was an only child, and as a boy he had to give up most boyhood pleasures to look after the home and his mother. He insisted that he had missed nothing, and that he only loved and admired his poor suffering mother. Now he was extremely upset about his wife's unkindness and aggressiveness to her. He had been attracted to his wife because she was so capable and active, qualities which he felt he lacked.

The wife was a tall, angular woman with somewhat masculine features, who dressed incongruously in bright colours and wore flowery hats—the only overt expression of her wish to be more feminine. She was a very sick woman who suffered from a congenital heart disease, just as her husband's mother did. She had two younger sisters who were pretty and feminine and very close to mother. She herself, unattractive physically, but intelligent, had always tried to ally herself with her father but was too delicate for 'boyish pursuits'. One can imagine her unconscious resentment against her mother who brought her into the world so ill-equipped and yet so dependent on her care, that the resentment was never allowed to come into consciousness.

In her marriage, she fought passionately and viciously against her husband's slowness and quietness, the very qualities she needed in him and in herself to cope with her delicate health. She drove herself into constant activity; her frequent violent outbursts naturally aggravated her illness.

During the therapeutic contact it became clear that the husband's own resentment and anger with his sick mother had been so incompatible with his love and concern for her that he could not tolerate it in himself. So he married a wife who could express it for him, and who unconsciously welcomed the opportunity to do so because of the unexpressed resentment towards her own mother. So what was expressed was a double dose, or even more, because as the husband had abdicated all his masculine aggression to her, she found herself manoeuvred, as it were, into expressing both her own and his anger. Their realization of these mechanisms during therapy, resulted in a remarkable lessening of the tension and distress both had felt. Indeed the wife's physical health improved remarkably, and the husband, no longer put off by her aggressive outbursts, became more masculine and able to stand up for himself.

Projections of disowned, repressed wishes, needs and drives onto the partner, and the mutually destructive processes which this may entail, can be seen as the underlying dynamics in a great many marital and family problems. The hardworking wife, who keeps herself, her home and her children meticulously clean and runs from agency to agency to complain about her dirty drunkard of a husband, may well be worried about the bad, dirty aspects of herself, perhaps her 'bad' sexuality. It may be this anxiety about herself which makes it so important for her to keep all the 'bad' things firmly fixed onto the husband. Her demands for help may express, on one level, an unconscious striving to relieve her of her guilt about herself which has been intolerably increased by her destructiveness towards her husband. Similarly, the rigid man with high moral standards who is desperately anxious about his slovenly, promiscuous or delinquent wife may need her to express similar drives of his own which he has never dared to face and has repressed into the unconscious.

Particularly instructive in this connection are cases where one 'well' partner brings an 'ill' husband or wife as 'the patient'. If one has the opportunity to work with such a case, it can often be seen that in spite of appearances to the contrary, the 'illness' is in fact shared between the two, the 'well' partner maintaining his well-being through the co-operation of the other partner who ostensibly carries the illness.

Not all couples marry with this need to project; many choose a partner as much like themselves as possible because they wish to identify and reinforce their image. Such marriages can be, and often are, happy and conflict-free, although they may be limited and limiting. The partners have rarely an overt marriage problem but may ask for help for difficulties with their children. For in such families the children may have to carry the projections of aspects of both parents' personalities which do not fit their mutually strengthened self-images. We shall talk about this more fully in Chapters 3, 4 and 5, which focus on the development of the children and their parents' response to its varying phases.

The second principle, or general way of looking at things, which guides our approach to understanding both marriage and human psychology in general, is that in lasting relationships, endowed with importance by their participants, there is usually a mutuality and complementarity in the needs, longings and fears that operate in the partnership. This is emphasized by the widespread, and in our view entirely accurate belief, that marital discord is usually the responsibility of both partners: 'It's six of one and a half dozen of the other.' It is our expectation that as we get to know a couple, we will find that there is a deeply unconscious 'agreement' as to the unwritten 'contract' of the marriage. Processes of interaction such as projection and identification are an integral part of this agreement. Its form is something like this: 'I will attempt to be some of the many important things you want of me, even though they are some of them impossible, contradictory and crazy, if you will be for me some of the important, impossible, contradictory and crazy things that I want of you. We don't have to let each other know what these thing are, but we will be cross, sulk, become depressed or difficult, if we do not keep to the bargain.' Once these deeply unconscious expectations of longings and fears have been established, although they are not immutable, they can be remarkably consistent.

Of course this second principle utilizes the first, in that we are making it clear that the 'agreement' is totally unconscious and usually employs projections also. For example, we discovered after a long contact with a couple, a familiar pattern of distress at the end of the working day. The husband would come in from work to find his wife angry and upset, and over the years she became bewildered and miserable because he would not be loving and considerate of her when he came home. Part of her unspoken and unconscious wish of him was that he should not get angry and withdraw from her in retaliation for the anger she felt against him because she felt envious of his freedom and deserted when he went off to work. The origin of this anger gradually became clear: in her childhood of this woman was a latch-key child; both her father and her mother worked full-time and she often felt deserted by them. To her it seemed that her husband was repeating this desertion daily when he left her to go to work. This example leads to the third principle on which we base our understanding of marriage, which is that many of the patterns of unconscious longings and fears that make up the unwritten marriage contract are derived from earlier and especially from infantile and childhood relationships. In the course of growing up, each person's emotional life is, we think, determined by intense longings for relationships with others. The particular nature of the relationship that is most intensely desired at each stage of life has qualities that are specifically date-stamped. Such longings can never, in our view, be completely met, but the more or less satisfactory meeting of needs and longings in each stage enables the person to satisfy the demands and needs of the next stage. To some extent, these longings are experienced directly and consciously but, especially after infancy, there will be a tendency for the longings in their original and most direct form, to become unconscious as their stridency and nature become less appropriate to the growing child, and less acceptable to the family and to socicty. Such unconscious longings are never really lost, we think, but can be reactivated quite regularly and normally in dreams and, remarkably, in the ability to appreciate the needs of infants and children. However, longings which were especially inadequately met or for unknown reasons were especially intense and insistent, are much more readily and frequently reactivated, and, throughout a person's emotional life they are more likely to be evident in some form or derivative as unconscious wishes and fantasies.

As the child grows out of infancy, he tends to take over as his own the needs and expectations that other people have of him, particularly the people who are important to him. Subsequently, in time, the person can be as loyal in pursuing the needs of these others as of his own wishes, longings and self-expectations.

Everyone, then, has within him a host of unconscious wishes and longings, derived from the different stages of development and characteristic of the different stages of life, and some of these unconscious needs are more important than others as motivating forces underlying the conscious needs of the individual in later phases of his life.

The principle that we are describing is that all of us have a tendency to get into repetitive patterns of relationships that are motivated by the persistence of wishes in unconscious fantasy form and derived from the way earlier needs were satisfied. Sometimes, in marriage, the repetitive aspect of sequences of partnership is remarkably literal, as when a woman whose childhood was damaged by her father's alcoholism, finds herself marrying a man who turns out to be an alcoholic, divorces him and then gets herself into the same situation once more. Or a man whose childhood was dominated by his mother's heart disease, may marry a woman with congenital heart trouble, as in the case just described.

In describing the life experiences of the people in our stories we will draw upon their childhood longings and the experiences of patterns of fulfilment of those longings. This leads us to the fourth and last of the principles we are enunciating here. This principle is that the pattern of relationships most commonly called to our minds in our work with families, couples and individuals, seems to derive from the time when the little child can realize something of the intensity of his own longings towards his parents whilst at the same time recognizing that the parents are themselves a couple with a particular and potentially intense relationship with each other from which the child is excluded. This is of course the situation already described as the oedipus complex. The way this group of experiences is patterned and evolves will crucially affect subsequent fantasies evoked by sexual longings for love affairs and marriage. Needs, longings and experiences from other parts of life will colour and shape the oedipal complex of longings and fears.

A family begins with a marriage. It is the literal matrix of the personalities of the children who grow up in that family, and being the children's most intense experience of this relationship will enormously influence the sort of marriage they themselves get into.

We shall, therefore, look at three examples of marriages which may illustrate the four principles, and especially the persistence of the oedipal theme and related secrets. This is the topic of our book.

The first story concerns *Mr and Mrs Cant*. Mrs Cant, a professional woman in her twenties, attractive and young looking, asked for help in great confusion. Three years earlier she had married a man who was much approved of by her family which consisted of her parents and a slightly older brother. Her marriage was now threatened because she had fallen in love with her brother's best friend. When she married, she had thought she was very much in love with her husband but now she could not bear him to get close to her. He was most upset and so was her family, who strongly disapproved of her extra-marital affair. They had no sympathy with her and sided entirely with her husband. Her boyfriend was reluctant to continue the relationship with her, as he did not want to be the cause of a marriage break-up, nor to lose the friendship of her brother and her parents. She felt that for both husband and boyfriend, the relationship with her family was more important than that with her. This raised the question whether for her too the relationship with her parental family was more important than with either man. She recalled that previous passionate love affairs had never lasted long as she lost interest in each lover once she got to know him well. She was worried that this pattern might be repeated with the present boyfriend.

To help with this confusion, Mr and Mrs Cant were offered individual therapeutic sessions. The husband accepted very reluctantly as he denied any need of help for himself. If his wife could give up her foolish selfish behaviour and listen to the advice given by him and her family, all was set for them to have a happy marriage. He complained that she never saw his point of view, and took little interest in his great hobby of vintage cars. He countered her complaint that he took no interest in her work at a day centre for handicapped children by saying that her preoccupation with this work was another expression of her selfish need to feel important.

It seemed that there was little good feeling left in this marriage which the wife compared deprecatingly with that of her parents. She described her own family as ideal, loving and supporting each other, united by interests and social causes which they jointly supported. The parents were very close and so was she to her brother. Her mother was proud of him and her father of her. She described their happy times together talking, listening to music and watching TV, when she used to sit at her father's feet while he stroked her hair. She asked herself whether the reason why she had not been able to maintain her previous relationships with men was that none of them had been as attractive as her father or her brother. She discovered that she had been interested only in men who would not attempt to break her strong tie with her family, but would help to strengthen it. Certainly her husband had made no attempt to help her to make a new family with him, but instead had adopted her family as his, seeming to welcome their constant invitations, phone calls and visits. The family lavished presents on her, with which her husband could not compete and her mother continued to choose and buy all Mrs Cant's clothes as she had done all her life. As Mrs Cant was talking about her ideal family, complicated mixed feelings began to emerge. She became aware not only of the tremendous rivalry between herself and her mother but also of the attempts on both sides to prevent hostility and mistrust between them ever coming into the open. Yet she rejoiced in the special friendships between 'her men' (boyfriends/husband) and her father and brother, a friendship which often led to the exclusion of her mother. She felt that the closeness between herself and her brother was sponsored by her mother and wondered whether this was so because the brother/sister relationship was less of a threat to the mother than her daughter's closeness to her father. Yet she also knew that her brother was attached to her and she to him for reasons of their own, and feared that her brother too would have great difficulty in finding a suitable partner. He introduced all his girlfriends to her for inspection, and then dismissed them.

Mr Cant did not find it easy to speak about his family which he saw as completely different from his wife's. They were conservative, rigid and avoided demonstrative feelings. The father was a disciplinarian, the mother highly-strung. Two married sisters were living abroad and there was little contact with them. He knew that he, the only son, was very important to his mother and felt guilty that he was not able to show her that he cared about her. He feared that any show of affection to her would result in open conflict with the father. The concern and outgoing warmth which his wife's family showed towards his own parents made him feel less guilty towards his own mother who he had deserted for their daughter. He had also hoped that this free and easy family might succeed where he had failed and help his parents to modify their rigid pattern. For all these reasons he colluded with the idealization of his wife's parents to the detriment of his own marriage and thus failed to help her in her opening moves towards a more realistic assessment of them.

Mr Cant, who had resisted using therapeutic help from the beginning, opted out of it after a few months but encouraged his wife to continue. Just as he had left it to his wife's family to do something about the conflict with his parents, he now left it to his wife to do something about the conflicts in his marriage. These centred more and more on his inability to support his wife in her attempts to become freer of her family. She used her therapy to achieve this and became able to share new insights with her husband. Slowly they began to feel themselves developing as a couple with the potential for a marriage, capable of maturing and becoming a family in their own right. This involved having more realistic attitudes towards their parental families.

Mrs Cant came to accept the futility of trying to replace her brother in an extra-marital affair and allowed herself to enjoy her sexual relationship with her husband. She recognized and overcame a feeling that she could not risk pregnancy because her parents would take over any child she had. The couple were, however, left wondering whether they might need to move abroad in order to build up an effective family life of their own.

When, a few weeks later, Mrs Cant did in fact become pregnant, and told the news to her parents, her mother's immediate response was: 'I shall have to give up my job to look after the baby.' The Cants were however able to tell the mother, firmly but kindly, that they wanted to look after the baby themselves.

Their case showed the bewilderment that in our view is so much the consequence of unconscious motivation in marriage. So far as they knew, they had married because they were in love and because they expected to bring themselves and each other happiness. Yet the close fit in the unconscious agreement in this marriage emerges very clearly. Mrs Cant's complicated wish to get away from the confusing feelings for her parents and her brother, and yet not get away, was met by Mr Cant's attraction to his wife's family. He saw it as an improvement on his own, (marrying to enter the partner's family is frequent, we think), but also as a corrective to his own family—a corrective which he had long wished for but had failed to supply himself. His idealization of his parents-in-law tended to confirm his wife in feeling that the ideal husband would be someone more like her father, rather than her own husband. Her marriage as well as her love affairs were a way of getting the closeness to her father that she wanted so much, whilst at the same time escaping the forbidden (because incestuous) aspects of her love for him. Her love affairs had to be impermanent because the lovers were meant to be substitutes for him, without succeeding in replacing him in her life.

It is quite possible that the instability which resulted from Mrs Cant's subsequent disillusion with him and her disruptive love affair, made her resemble in her husband's mind his nervous and vulnerable mother, and hence presented him with the possibility of entering into a new version of the son-mother relationship of his childhood. He hoped (unconsciously) to achieve in adulthood what he could not achieve earlier—to make a woman feel better through his love.

They had been as we have seen, strongly supported in their choice of each other by their respective families who each felt, quite accurately, that the chosen partner would not estrange their son or daughter from them but share and reinforce the existing family ties.

We have chosen this story, as we have most of the other examples in this book, because it illustrates the principles we see as being important about human relationships. Moreover the stories are chosen for their aptness, but few of the cases strike us as being very unusual or unrepresentative of our general experience.

Mr and Mrs Dalton had, in contrast to the Cants, married each other in spite of strong disapproval of both sets of parents who justifiably felt that their son's and daughter's choice of a marriage partner representing extreme opposite views to their own, was an affront and a rejection. In their choice of each other, the young couple moved both geographically and in their life style as far away from the parental families as possible. Each had chosen the partner because he/she appeared to be completely different from the parent of the opposite sex for whom they felt a curious mixture of love, fear and identification. They also shared feelings of contempt and guilt for the parent of the same sex. These shared conflicting feelings kept them, against their conscious wishes, fettered to their parents, and strongly affected their marriage.

They asked for help after eight years of marriage because they were still childless. Both longed to have children but although the wife conceived easily, she had had several miscarriages and one premature stillborn child. No physical causes could be found, and the couple's anxiety had led to the husband's frequent premature ejaculations, and the wife's angry sexual withdrawal. Mrs Dalton blamed their childlessness entirely on her husband's impaired potency. She saw him as a weakling, utterly different from her father. That he nevertheless made her feel intellectually inferior to him, as her father had done, increased her fury. Mr Dalton, who had early in his marriage perceived his wife as a charming gentle girl, now saw her as an unmanageable virago. He was as afraid of her as he had been of his mother, and although she was totally unlike his mother, in an odd way he felt her now to be just the same.

In spite of all the conflicts, the Dalton's marriage had rich and warm aspects. After a short period of therapy, during which both partners were able to realize consciously some of the unconscious determinants of their behaviour, Mrs Dalton became pregnant again. This time she was able to complete her pregnancy and have a healthy baby, and two years later they had a second child.

The experiences of the Cants and the Daltons demonstrate that neither the conscious wish to identify with the parents, nor the conscious wish to repudiate them, enables a young couple to become free of unconscious and conflicting bonds to their parents, which therefore continue to hinder them from developing their own specific potential as marriage partners and as parents. They need to understand, accept and work through some of their ambivalent feelings towards their parental families so that they can enjoy without fear in their marriage feelings and longings which were first aroused in their relationship with the parent of the opposite sex but forbidden and therefore unfulfilled.

The final example of this chapter which concerns *Mr and Mrs Bryant* shows particularly well the importance of the oedipal theme. This couple fell in love with each other at a point in both their lives when their oedipally derived needs were especially pressing. Although initially they seemed to be offering to each other some hope of re-experiencing and perhaps of mastering their oedipal difficulties, they became, as we shall see, trapped by the repetition.

They had been married five years when they asked for help as their marriage was on the point of breaking. It was the husband who initiated the request, as he was deeply distressed by his wife's threat to leave him.

The couple had met in Rhodesia, the wife's home. The husband had travelled there with his sick mother who wanted to visit relatives. She was a beautiful and possessive woman, and he, her only child, was born after the death of his father, a gifted artist worshipped by his wife. After his death she transferred this worship on to her son who was made to feel so much a part of her that he could not be free to be himself. He was small and delicate but appealing in appearance, lacked vitality and was very shy. Academically he worked well and hard but had few interests beyond his studies, hardly any friends and no girlfriend at all. Under the shadow of his mother's terminal illness he fell in love with the lively and attractive girl who represented life to him and whom he saw as the opposite of his mother. They married soon after his mother's death much against her parents' (especially her father's) wishes.

After their marriage the couple went back to England, and moved into his mother's house. He insisted that everything there had to remain as it was, and criticized his wife, who had an exacting profession of her own, for not keeping the house as his mother had done. The wife felt that he did not see her as a real person with her own identity and refused to live with a husband who seemed more in touch with his dead mother than with his living wife. She also felt that while he had been so attracted by her liveliness and ability to make friends, he now resented and envied these very qualities. When she threatened to leave him he was desperate but seemed unable to change his attitudes, and they decided on a trial separation. The wife enjoyed her freedom, started friendships and love affairs with several men but became increasingly puzzled why she always picked men who were overclose to their mothers. Initially she denied that this might indicate some tie-up with her parents and insisted that they had nothing to do with the present situation. It took some time before she could talk about her family.

Her father was a well known explorer, tall, good-looking, exciting but often away from home, his wife and two daughters. Mrs Bryant saw her mother as dull, conventional and limited but was most upset when her father left her for another woman, a divorcee with two daughters. He married this woman at the point when Mrs Bryant's own marriage was breaking but took the trouble to come to England to see her. At this meeting it became clear how important and how frightening their relationship had been to both of them. The father revealed that ever since her adolescence he had been torn between his wish to be close to this daughter and his anxiety that he might become too close. He had opposed her marriage because he sensed that it was mainly an attempt to escape from him and that a husband who was so utterly different from himself and from her background would not bring her happiness. Mrs Bryant in turn, was able to face after this meeting the realization that the choice of a husband so totally unlike her father had been intended to banish her father from her sexual fantasies; she realized too, that her husband had chosen her for the same reason in relation to his mother.

From early childhood she had refused to identify with her mother. She had become an interesting, lively personality in identification with her father but had always felt guilty about the seductive component in her personality and her secret wish to have her father to herself. When he left her mother she felt partly to blame.

Mr Bryant, like many posthumously born children, had been the recipient of feelings which belonged to the much admired lost partner whom he felt compelled to replace for his mother but failed to do so. He had always felt that he had death inside him and that he lacked the strength to battle with life. Jean Paul Sartre,[25] a famous posthumous child, describes in his autobiography *Words* his preoccupation with similar feelings throughout his young adulthood.

Although consciously Mr and Mrs Bryant were attracted to each other, the unconscious components in their choice, their fantasies about their parents, made it impossible for them to relate realistically to each other. An oedipal collusion of this type can be seen in varying degrees of intensity as the motif for many, perhaps most marriages, and it can become the basis for very satisfactory fulfilling relationships. What needs to be fulfilled is the wish to enjoy in relation to the partner what could not be fulfilled in relation to the parent, because it was forbidden, threatening and guilt-laden. The partner can represent some aspect of the desired parent but as, in fact, he is not the parent, the relationship can be enjoyed without oppressive guilt. The ability to symbolize is one condition for joyful fulfilment.

3. Making room for the baby in the family

The reader will have seen that our main concern is less with the individual member of a family than with the complex inter-relationships of the family as a whole. We are trying to understand these by looking at the expectations and anxieties, which on both a conscious and an unconscious level, determine the roles given by family members to each other, and influence the situation in the whole family. This approach is especially important for this chapter in which we explore what the coming of the baby means in our contemporary urban society with its small families. Social changes have largely done away with the extended family structure, in the past a great support to new parents. Government services have been developed to compensate for its disappearance. Hospital facilities are now used for the majority of confinements, and there is careful preparation on a practical level for expectant mothers, and increasingly also for fathers. But birth, like death, is full of mystery, and no practical preparation will touch the secret fears and fantasies of mothers and fathers about the birth itself, and about what their baby will be like and what it will mean to them.[26]

In spite of our attempts to see the coming of the baby against the wider background of the family, we have to acknowledge that in this family drama there are two chief actors: the newborn infant and its mother.

They are a vulnerable pair: the infant, who is only just beginning to exist as an individual, and the mother, who during part of her pregnancy and after the birth of her child is in that special condition which D. W. Winnicott[27] calls 'primary maternal pre-occupation'. Perhaps because the special place of infant and mother is so obvious, there has been little study of other participants in the scene which the coming of the baby inevitably changes, although in recent years the father has been acknowledged both psychologically and socially as a major participant. For example, he is now offered opportunities to feel included in many antenatal clinics,

is encouraged to take part in the courses there and often also to
be present during the confinement. Many fathers may feel under
pressure to accept these arrangements even though they may
sense a lack of welcome from staff and mothers when they arrive
at the clinic. The aim throughout is to increase their understanding
of how to help the mother on a practical level during pregnancy
and confinement and after the baby's birth, but still the emphasis
is always on the mother and the baby, offering little opportunity
for the father to explore his own feelings, nor for the couple to
anticipate the great task of giving up their exclusive two-person
relationship. For both of them, this task will evoke the feelings
stemming from their earliest experiences of having to share their
mother in their own infancy. But while the new mother can re-
capture the sense of a close twosome in relation to her baby, the
new father will have to cope with a feeling of loss until the family
can, by finding a place for him, create a new three-person relationship. The degree to which each partner has or has not succeeded
in coping with this same task in childhood will be reflected in the
adult couple's capacity to re-adapt to the new situation. Difficulties
may occur if one partner refuses to allow a third person into the
relationship. Such a refusal will usually be unconscious, and might
be expressed, for instance, in a husband's excessive anxiety about
the dangers to his wife during confinement. His terror of 'losing
her' may in fact be his fear of losing her exclusive love.

The loss of the precious twosome may also be anticipated with
sorrow by the wife. We may illustrate this point by describing a
couple who both came from large families. The wife had never felt
secure in the love of her mother, who was an ambitious and competitive woman and felt her daughters as rivals. The husband, on
the other hand, had the sort of maternal mother who could embrace
all her many children and could share them with her husband.
On the eve of her first confinement, the wife, full of anxious anticipation about what the birth of the baby would mean, said to her
husband: 'Do you realize that this is the end of what is most
precious to us? Never again shall we have our treasured twosome.'
He, caressing her, replied: 'The more love we give, the more love
we shall have.'

The couple's relationship to each other will affect their feelings
about the coming of the baby as well as the wife's capacity to be a
mother, and both are conditioned by each partner's own experience

of having been mothered. This in turn depends on the relationship between the parents of each partner.

For the new mother it is important to feel that in the twosome between her and her baby, upon which the baby's growth depends, the baby's father need not be excluded; that they can support each other in making her 'primary maternal pre-occupation' manageable without guilt or resentment, and with great joy.

To offer children wholesome ground for growth, parents have not only to feel sufficiently secure in themselves and in each other, but also to be able to acknowledge their mixed feelings about the new demands made on them. This is not easy in our society in which the birth of a baby is proclaimed as a wonderful event, and new parents are expected to radiate happiness. The fortunate couple to whom a healthy thriving baby is born will soon forget their fears and trepidations, but during pregnancy all couples have anxious moments about what their baby will be like and what it will mean to their lives. These may be hard for them to admit; it may be harder still to share with each other their negative feelings about the inevitable changes in their lives.

Now that a generation of fathers is growing up who want to participate in the baby's birth and growth, (a wish which was considered quite inappropriate by the generation of their fathers), communication between the couple is becoming easier. It also helps that mothers are better informed and can feel themselves to be in greater control of a creative act. Yet many of a couple's unconscious fears, stemming from childhood beliefs about the birth of babies, are not allayed by straightforward information.

Some couples try to maintain a unisex image after the baby is born, either by the father pretending to assume the role of the mother and taking over the baby, or by trying to ignore its existence. One such couple placed the baby's cot as far away from their own room as possible and reported proudly: 'Our baby is so good, we don't see or hear anything of him. It is just as if he wasn't there.'

However much a woman desires a child, there will be some negative aspects which have to be faced in pregnancy and motherhood. The pregnancy irrefutably commits her to being a woman and a mother, and any half-conscious fantasy that expresses her unwillingness for these roles has to be renounced.

In the past, when a girl was educated in anticipation of her maternal role, it involved less of a change in her life than it does for the modern 'liberated' woman who has a job or career. Marriage is no longer the great dividing line, because the young wife continues much of her previous life and shares her husband's interests. The real change comes with the arrival of the baby, when she may be full of anxiety about how good a mother she can be and about her ability to adapt to her fundamentally changed role of primarily a housewife and mother. Also she is unused to being dependent on her husband for money, which may anyhow become short when there is only one source of income.

Frequently, young women who have been independent, having had their own work or career, get carried away by the idealization of motherhood and are pining to have a baby.[28] They persuade their husbands to start a family sooner than was originally planned, and may be radiant throughout the pregnancy. But when the fantasies about having a lovely baby and being a cherished wife and mother are not matched by the reality, they feel angry and frustrated, 'trapped' and 'tied' or like 'cows who supply milk' and only their sense of duty and fear of disapproval stops them from running away. After a few months, when the baby becomes a person who rewards them with smiles and gives them pleasure, these women's attitudes may change and they may become doting mothers.

A mother's reaction may also be the reverse. She may adore her tiny baby with whom she still identifies as part of herself, but when the baby turns into a toddler with a wilful personality presenting never-ending and often aggressive demands, and an occasional preference for the father who begins to play his part in the child's life, she may revolt against motherhood. She may be determined not to remain 'just a suburban housewife', and use the first opportunity to find a childminder or nursery.

The frequency of depression in mothers during the weeks or months following childbirth has been widely acknowledged and discussed, for example by Peter Lomas.[29]

'Most surveys have not looked at the effect of having children on the prevalence of depression but there is some evidence that women with young children have particularly high rates of depression. Two community surveys in two different London Boroughs using a clinical interview to identify the presence of depression found rates of between 26 and 40 per cent of women with young children (Brown et al,[30] 1975; Richman[31] 1976).'

It seems clear that the more the mother can allow the father to participate in the baby's care, and the more the father can enjoy doing so, the less likely is the mother's isolation and depression, and the greater the prospect for the family's general welfare and happiness. It is just because the father is somehow more distant that he has an important role to play, and may be able to spot the right moment for a change in the daily routine. *Bella*, a healthy and happy two year old, had been reliably dry during the day for some time but was still given a nappy at night as a matter of course. One night when her father was putting her to bed, he asked: 'Do you still want a nappy?' 'No, I don't,' replied the child. The mother was anxiously anticipating a wet bed, but from that night on, Bella never again needed a bed-time nappy.

Some mothers, who adore little babies but who find themselves in difficulties with toddlers, may go on becoming pregnant to fulfil their need to have a compliant baby who satisfies their intense longing for a dependent relationship. Such a mother can be the despair of the family planning clinic and may well rear a problem family.

There are other ambivalent attitudes towards motherhood. So-called 'liberated' women, when pregnant, may express in different ways contradictory feelings which they have not been able to resolve, both towards motherhood and towards their jobs. They may not feel sufficiently supported and understood in either aspect of their lives by their husbands. But if the mother can share her feelings with the father, and he with her his fears of being excluded, then they may be able together to manage their difficulties and begin to enjoy the pleasures of parenthood. Working wives who have been successful in gratifying jobs are likely to plan and approach motherhood more realistically. Even if—in the age of Spock and Bowlby—they see motherhood as a full-time occupation, at least for some time.

The new mother who is able and willing to talk about confusion and fears, may do so with a trusted person, perhaps a friend, health visitor or doctor to whom this may be a familiar and readily understood situation and who can give her support and encouragement. The new father's response receives less attention. He may have his own anxieties about being a good enough father to his child and husband to his wife, who needs his special love and support at a time when he himself may be jealous and guilty about his contradictory feelings. He knows more about the importance of his feelings and attitudes in both these relationships than the former generation of fathers did, but how far is jealousy both of his wife's ability to have a baby and of the baby itself understood and acknowledged? In his studies about puerperal depression, Peter Lomas[32] found a close connection between the husband's lack of support for his wife's mothering and the frequency and severity of the illness. What help, then, does the father need to be able to give the necessary support?

Most new mothers feel close to their own mothers with whom they can now share the secrets of motherhood. If they have an image of a 'good' mother this relationship will help towards the necessary adjustment, although it may hinder it where there have been very mixed feelings towards the mother. Does the new father similarly attempt to get reinforcement for his paternal feelings from his father by identifying with him? Does he ever feel that he and his father can share fatherhood secrets? Or is he more likely to turn to his mother in identification with the baby he once was to her? Or in identification with his wife who now is a mother? These and other similar questions still need investigation.

In some primitive societies the husband who has labour pains while his wife is in labour has a couvade, a lying-in bed, as his wife does. Although this can be seen as a means to get attention, it may also be a claim to prove paternity. He seems to be saying: 'Look at me, having cramps and ailments at the same time as my wife: surely that proves that I am the father of the baby she produces.'

In our society the father can get his couvade only in a roundabout way, becoming an object of jokes for others and of shame for himself. A man who worked in a war hospital in Cyprus started such severe stomach cramps while making a patient's bed, that he had to be confined to bed for twenty-four hours. He was 'cured' when a wire arrived telling him of the birth of a healthy baby girl in a maternity hospital in Devon. As the baby was born a week before the expected time, this husband's symptoms were apparently an intuitive response to the event and not to an anticipated date.

Another husband who had slighty resented the tremendous fuss made of his wife during her first confinement, fractured his pelvis after the birth of his second child, and so was now also entitled to special attention.

Typical of many such stories is that of a medical consultant who was much looking forward to the birth of his first baby, and had insisted on sharing all preparations with his wife. He attended antenatal classes and arranged to stay with her throughout the confinement. At the onset of labour he drove her to the hospital, and upon entering the building he started such a heavy nosebleed that all the attention of the staff went to him and nobody had time for his wife. Everybody working in this field knows similar stories, always told in a patronizing way, implying that the father is wholly childish and has no right to the feelings which underlie these anecdotes.

Even relatively mature and co-operative husbands often complain bitterly that they don't count once their wives are pregnant. 'Everybody now only enquires about my wife, nobody wants to know how I am', and 'When the baby comes I will be completely left out.' Yet many men fit in with the general attitude that having a baby is a woman's affair. They get particularly busy at work during the later phases of their wife's pregnancy and during their baby's infancy. By making sure of using their 'demanding' jobs to avoid getting involved, they are playing into the mother's ambivalence about sharing the baby with the father.

There are also men who always manage to be away when it comes to the confinement. One such man disappeared on the day of his first child's birth for six weeks, and arranged to enlist in the army just before the birth of his second child. Other men get drunk or go out with prostitutes while their wives are in labour. Probation officers frequently mention husbands who become delinquent and go to prison when their wives are having babies. On the other hand very narcissistic men may get great satisfaction and excitement from their baby's birth and go on talking about it at great length, often without even mentioning their wives. It sounds as if it were their single-handed achievement. These examples of fathers' responses may appear to be contradictory, but they all show how much the father is reacting to the birth of his baby and how great is his need to have his involvement acknowledged. If this could be accepted as natural and without shame, the more infantile expressions of it could perhaps be avoided.

It is difficult in our western society for a man to come to terms with his childishness and with his envy of the womb and of the woman. We talk light-heartedly about the girl's envy of the man, about penis envy, encourage little girls to be tomboys and adult women to compete with men in all areas of life; but the little boy who plays with dolls causes raised eyebrows. Girls can be dressed like boys but when the little boy wants to wear his sister's dress there is anxiety—'Is he going to be a transvestite?'—and if he resents his sister wearing his trousers he is made to feel mean.

The birth of a baby not only emphasizes the difference between the sexes and the feelings aroused by these differences, it also creates a crisis—as do all transitions from one stage of life to another. All the major crisis-points of life, as well as making progression possible, also stimulate regression; yet young parents are supposed to meet the arrival of their baby with increased maturity, and if they behave childishly, wanting to be babied themselves, they feel guilty, disapproved of, a failure.

It is generally acknowledged that new mothers have to cope with tremendous demands and they can expect tolerance and support especially during the first weeks and during the breast feeding period. Fathers are not supposed to show any symptoms of a baby trauma but to act maturely and take responsibility from the moment of the baby's birth.

Breast feeding, which gives most mothers deep satisfaction and is for many people a moving, almost 'religious' experience to watch, may have different implications for the father. There appears to be something like a taboo preventing him from handling his wife's breasts during the breast feeding period. This he may feel acutely as a deprivation especially as at this time his own erotic feelings about the breasts are usually greatly stimulated. So, too, are more unconscious feelings reawakened, oral incestuous fantasies about his mother, which may make him want to share the baby's milk and suck the mother's breast. However, the wife's feelings about her body have changed and her breasts, which she may previously have felt as sexual organs to be enjoyed as part of the love-play with her husband, have now become a primary source of giving satisfaction to her baby. She may feel repelled by her husband's wish to be a rival to the baby if he wants to continue to use her breasts as a source of erotic pleasure for himself. If apparently infantile attitudes could be acknowledged as natural and acceptable, they might become integrated with the more mature aspects of the personality without guilt or shame.

How difficult this can be, is shown by the story of a successful professional man, married to a woman twenty years younger than himself. He asked for help for his marriage, accusing his wife of promiscuous attention-seeking behaviour, but was half aware that he might provoke her failings by his superior attitudes, by always sitting 'in the Chair'. In a joint session with his own and his wife's therapists the couple's usual roles were rapidly reversed, and the wife appeared to be the more mature of the two. She said she had always known that husbands were often envious of their babies and made mothering difficult for their wives, but had thought that this could not happen to her, as she had a husband so much older and so greatly superior. In fact, however, he was worse than any other husband she knew. While she was speaking, the 'superior' husband had been sliding down in his chair and was sucking his thumb. The therapists acknowledged his difficulty in integrating the baby inside himself with his important and highly successful professional life. In the night following this session, this man could for the first time openly bring his baby-needs to his wife and she could respond by lovingly mothering him. From then on she became also more able to acknowledge his achievements and his strength with less envy and resentment.

The case of *John Ellis* illustrates the difficulties of one young father. A married man of twenty-four, he was referred for treatment after a second incident of delinquent behaviour, which seemed to be out of keeping with his otherwise impeccable record. He had been ostentatiously flirting with an assistant in the grocery shop where he was the manager, presenting her with bits of jewellery which he had stolen from his mother-in-law. The girl lived next door to his wife's relatives, and he would take her home after work and kiss and cuddle her in front of the house, obviously wanting to be found out. When he was, his wife was deeply upset and threatened to divorce him. They had been married for a year and she was three months pregnant. John was an only son, with two much older sisters, and had always been his mother's darling. On the outbreak of the war he was called up and accepted into a Guards regiment. Soon after, his mother had a stroke and died a few months later. John always felt that she had died because he had left her. As a P.T. instructor in the army he became especially friendly with his sergeant, a young married man, who was worried because he had left his young wife alone at home. When John's mother died and his father too was left alone and needed looking after, the two men between them arranged that the sergeant's wife should move into the father's house. On his first home leave John was worried by the close relationship between his father and the sergeant's young wife. His suspicions were confirmed when a few months later the woman was found to be pregnant by his father, and her husband divorced her. By the time John was discharged from the army, there was a baby a few months old, and he felt intense guilt for having helped to make this arrangement which had destroyed his sergeant's marriage and violated his mother's memory. He got a job at a tobacconist's, and after a few months was arrested for having robbed the till. He did it in such a clumsy way that it seemed as if he wanted to be found out and punished, and to get away from the painful situation at home. He achieved this through a short prison sentence.

After his discharge John got a job in a grocer's shop, left home, and married. His wife was an only daughter, her only brother having been killed in the war. She almost consciously chose John as a substitute son for her parents, and he was warmly welcomed by them as such. The mother became particularly fond of him, to the great delight of the father, a self-employed builder, who had always been very close to his daughter. Now the balance in this family seemed to be restored. As a wedding present the father built a house for the young couple near his own home, and spent all his spare time improving and decorating it, even after they had moved in. It became 'his house' and John often felt excluded. When his wife became pregnant, her father was overjoyed and immediately started to make a cot for 'our baby'. The father-in-law's attitude painfully re-activated in John the incestuous fantasies which were aroused when his father had had a baby by a young woman of his daughter's age. Once again John responded destructively because of his confusion about mothers and lovers, and his envy and jealousy of the woman who could have a baby.

When the young couple went into therapy, the husband, who was very masculine in appearance, would demonstrate to his therapist, (an elderly woman), on his own body the changes which occurred in his wife's body as the pregnancy progressed: the big breasts, the swelling tummy. He made it clear that his delinquency was an expression of his need to steal the baby from his wife, for he wanted to be the creative mother himself.

When the baby was born he carried him round with a pride which seemed to say, 'He is mine; I've made him.'

A new baby may stimulate baby-needs in either parent, and a man's identification and competition with the baby may make it difficult for him to assume the role of a father. Frequently, too, stress develops if a husband identifies his wife with his mother.

'Any man whose awareness of women still refers directly to his experience with his mother, and who has not been able to see relations with other women as a symbolic, and therefore acceptable, way of securing her for himself, suffers considerable inhibitions in his sexual life. In his unconscious mind his wife is his mother, and his behaviour with his spouse is inhibited by the taboo appropriate only to the idea of having sexual relations with one's mother. It is common for a couple to find that difficulties of this kind either first appear or, if already present, became greatly exacerbated, when the first child is born. The wife comes to share even more properties and roles of the man's own mother, making it harder still for him to distinguish between the original object of his emotion and its present-day substitute.'[33]

This excerpt may explain the frequent deterioration of sexual relations, caused by the husband's inhibitions which make him turn away from his wife, or his actual impotence, after the birth of a baby. If this can be understood and talked about, much unhappiness may be avoided.

Parents may use a child from the moment of birth as extensions of themselves, and assign roles to him or her which fit their own fantasies rather than the personality of the child. The case histories of eighteen-year-old *Janet* and nine-year-old *Peter* show this. They also help us to remain aware of the three generation cycle in families for grandparents, directly or indirectly via the parents, affect the lives of their grandchildren. Janet's and Peter's parents were still dominated by their ambivalent feelings towards their parents and this contributed much towards their inability to relate to their own children realistically, and the children's symptoms in their turn, drew attention to the parents' need for help.

Janet Read, a beautiful and intelligent girl of eighteen, was in danger of becoming a drug addict. The girl was in psychiatric treatment and her therapist felt that her parents, especially her mother, for whom Janet had been from birth an extension of herself, needed some help.

This mother was the only daughter of a woman who was a confusing mixture of a powerful professional woman and a greedy child, and who rejected all feminine tasks. Her father, weak and ineffective in many ways, was the one who ran the house, did the cooking and much of the mothering. *Mrs Read* had been a delicate baby and had had considerable feeding difficulties. She felt throughout her childhood that her mother only cared for her when she was ill but otherwise rejected her, especially in her femininity, and she blamed her for her lack of it. Her mother's overeating and disgusting eating habits repelled Mrs Read and she herself never took any interest in food or cooking.

She married an attractive, artistic and delicate man. He had been the only son of a possessive mother, towards whom he had a most ambivalent relationship. He was very finicky about food, especially about food which was offered to him, as if he needed to have it very much under his own control. On the other hand he liked to cook, was good at it, and could enjoy the meals he had prepared himself. When Janet was born, her mother never stopped feeding her. Until the child was a year old, she was day and night at her mother's breast. *Mr Read* was completely excluded both as a father and as a husband. Janet became a beautiful and successful child, the fulfilment of her mother's dreams, the attractive female, which she herself had never been able to be. Mrs Read loved making Janet look beautiful, enjoyed buying dresses for her —while she could never be bothered about her own appearance and resented her husband spending money on clothes for her.

All went well until Janet reached puberty. Up to then she had shone at school, now she began playing truant, lost interest and mixed with a crowd of drop outs whom she would bring home without her parents' consent. Her first serious boyfriend was a heroin addict, and at sixteen she left home to live with him.

Her mother remained completely identified with her, went through agonies and lived through all Janet's symptoms as if they were her own, At one point when Janet was back at the parental home, trying to wean herself from drugs, she started overeating and putting on weight. Her mother became frantic and could hardly bring herself to provide food for her. On another occasion, when the weaning attempts had broken down and Janet needed money to buy drugs, she became delinquent and promiscuous. Her mother was at that point tortured by delinquent and sexual fantasies of her own.

As time went on, the importance of her father for Janet became increasingly clear, and he responded willingly to her need for his attention and concern which met his own need to care for and be acknowledged by her.

Although it was on one level a relief for her mother that the father was now prepared to take some responsibility for Janet, she found it extremely difficult to share her with him. Indeed all three, Janet, father and mother, wanted exclusive twosomes, and had apparently never been able to cope with a three-person-relationship. The father could only effectively help Janet if he had her to himself; the mother, although aware of Janet's need for her father, often sabotaged their relationship; and Janet became upset and got into renewed trouble on the few occasions when the parents went on a holiday together.

It was only after Janet had stayed for two years at a drug addiction centre where she had been accepted on the condition that there would be no contact with her parents, and where in fact she was cured, that some degree of separation and of sharing became possible in this family.

Janet's parents were in most aspects of their personalities extreme opposites, but had similar difficulties about food and about sharing, stemming from their earliest relationships. There was much that they valued in each other, but neither was able nor willing to modify those attitudes which were harmful to the other partner and to Janet, who was deeply emotionally involved with them both. This eldest child, a girl, had to carry the burden of the parent's shared fantasies about greed and food, about exclusive love and sexuality. A few years later when the Reads had a son, he was left much freer from the parents' projections, perhaps because all the emotional pressure in this family was centred on femininity. The mother had rejected her own; the father, albeit unconsciously and guiltily, cherished his feminine features, and both shared a fantasy of Janet as the ideal woman. Their anxieties about femininity and the food phobias were unconsciously expected to be 'made good' by Janet, who was compulsively overfed as a baby and made into a seductive woman in adolescence. She rejected both these expectations, by acting them out in the most destructive way.

Peter Miller was nine years old when his school referred him to a child guidance clinic after his parents, *Mr and Mrs Miller* had pestered them for months with their anxiety about him. According to them he was disobedient, would refuse to do anything that 'normal boys' did, and worst of all, was sure to become a delinquent, as on several occasions he had stolen a few coins from his mother's purse.

The boy went to the same school as his sister *Mary* who was three years older. She was more successful in every respect: she was taller and stronger physically, an ambitious hard-working girl who always came top of her class. She was good at games and had already decided to train as a P.T. mistress. Peter, in contrast, hated physical exercise; to his parents' disgust, his one great interest was cooking.

The clinic's social worker, who had an interview with both parents, felt that their anxiety about Peter was out of proportion to the boy's disturbance or shortcomings. She described the father, who was a storekeeper and scoutmaster as passive and withdrawn, and extremely concerned that his boy was not manly enough and had little initiative. The mother, who spoke and behaved like a shy little girl, nevertheless expressed great ambition for her family, which so far only Mary, the eldest, gave any signs of fulfilling. Her main complaint of Peter was that she could never make him do what she wanted, and she was frantic that he would turn out to be a delinquent, and a thief.

Peter was offered individual sessions with a male therapist. The social worker invited both parents for weekly meetings in which it soon emerged that Mary was not the husband's child. She had been conceived when her mother was very young, as the result of a love-affair with her first employer, a married man. Mrs Miller had been very unhappy at home. She could not get on with her mother by whom she felt always criticized and made to feel stupid. With her father she had a 'secret understanding' but her mother 'killed it in the bud' and always stood between her and her father. The affair with the first employer was almost consciously an attempt to get some love from a father substitute. And indeed it was her real father who stood up for his daughter when she became pregnant, insisted that she must stay at home and made much fuss of the baby when she was born. He could show his grandchild the affection which his wife had not allowed him to show openly to his daughter.

The grandmother, too, enjoyed looking after her daughter's baby, while the young mother went out to work—but she longed to get away from home as the situation there made her most uneasy. She was therefore delighted to accept the proposal of Mr Miller to marry her and adopt the now six-months-old Mary. He was a little younger, an only child. His father had been in the army when he was born and when he came home after the war, he felt the boy who was very close to his mother, as an intruder. His mother alternated between favouring and rejecting her son, who became increasingly insecure and was longing to get away from home and have a family of his own to which he could safely belong. And until Peter was born all went well. But Peter was from the start difficult and delicate, so different from the sunny, healthy baby Mary had been. His parents were always worried about him and began to blame each other for his weediness and the fact that he was not as good as Mary. Mr Miller blamed his wife for not being a good-enough mother, not as good as his own mother had been, or indeed Mary's grandmother who had looked after her. And Mrs Miller blamed her husband for not being much of a man, so different from Mary's father, or her own, or her brothers. She also felt that her mother despised her for having such a weakly little boy when her own two sons had been strapping and full of vitality.

These parents' anxieties about Peter were an expression of their anxieties about themselves. They behaved to Peter in the same critical and doubting way as they felt her mother and his father respectively had behaved to them. Mary, who had an illegitimate father and who had been mothered by Mrs Miller's mother, could be loved and valued. They had no doubt that she would be a success and had no apparent guilt about her illegitimacy. This became all the more puzzling when it emerged that soon after Mary's birth her natural father was convicted for fraud and had to serve a prison sentence. But all the guilt and anxiety which might have been raised in relation to Mary was directed towards Peter. In their first legitimate child these parents saw all that worried them in themselves. To them he was an expression of their own inadequacy and especially of their weak, guilty, infantile sexuality. They spoke of 'playing about' with each other, chasing each other through house and garden. They could hardly believe that this 'playing about' could result in producing a baby. When it did, they doubted from the beginning that this baby could ever grow into a proper boy.

In their sessions with the social worker, Mr and Mrs Miller were able to see and put into words much of this. The fact that Peter's therapist liked and valued the boy increased his value in their eyes, and helped them to see him more realistically. They also discovered that Peter had some of those qualities which they had to an extent cherished in themselves but had not dared to develop, because they were disapproved of by their parents. They too had been 'dreamy', full of imagination, liked to read and to draw—all such 'useless' things! When they began to value them in Peter, and withdrew some of their negative projections from him, he appeared to become a much more lovable boy for them.

Mary, too, began to change. The girl who had been rather a prig, having to be so faultless and wonderful, became more relaxed, less bossy in the home and to Peter. How this change in atmosphere affected him could be seen in new achievements at school and elsewhere. His parents ceased to worry that his only real interest was cooking. They began to feel that this might not be such a disaster. They might, they thought, afford to send him to Switzerland and train as a chef. In fact, however, Peter later became a successful engineer.

When the parents married, they were still so closely identified with their own parents that they related to their children, especially Peter, the first child of their marriage, as their parents had related to them. Because they had been unable to develop their own identity as parents they made it impossible for Peter to develop his own identity—to be 'himself'. Their 'shared fantasies' stemming from their oedipal collusion, had attracted them to each other but had also stopped them from attaining greater maturity. They both needed a new experience with a 'parental figure' whose awareness of the child in each of them would enable them to make this development. This is the main therapeutic task in cases where problems present themselves primarily in parental roles.

Such changes are not necessarily achieved only in a therapeutic setting. The therapeutic task of 're-parenting'—providing a renewed opportunity to engage in a quasi-parent-child relationship for those whose first experience of it has been unsuccessful or incomplete—is not necessarily a professional job. Unless there is too much disturbance or rigidity, a therapeutic personality in a real life situation, perhaps a good neighbour, a wise relative or colleague, might have done the same job.

Peter's development was affected by the special position which his sister Mary held in the family. Whenever a baby is born into a family in which there are already other children, the feelings about the newcomer will depend on many factors: the size of the existing family, age difference and sex will obviously play a part, but so will less rational factors, mostly unconscious. The child who has the same position in the family as the parent has had, or whose conception and birth recall joyful or painful memories, or whose sex is not the expected and wanted one, will have special meaning for the parents and bring about special responses.

A beloved first-born boy had eighteen months later a brother who died in infancy. When he saw the dead baby on his crying mother's lap he had a minor fit. Similar fits recurred throughout his adult life whenever he was under emotional strain. He became outstandingly successful in his profession, was happy in his marriage and had one adored daughter. His wife wanted more children but he refused. The guilty memory of his dead baby brother made it impossible for him to consider a second child.

Another man, who had spent a few weeks in a hospital isolation ward at the age of three, just at the time when his mother gave birth to a second baby, became a loving father to his first child from the moment of birth but had great difficulty in relating lovingly to his second child. He could not help identifying it with the brother he felt had usurped his place in his childhood family.

A health visitor referred to a therapist a woman who had been an excellent mother to her first baby daughter but had tried to suffocate her second baby. Her first remark was: 'I never wanted her, I always only wanted the three of us, Betty, my husband and myself.' In deepest distress her story unfolded; she had been a happy only child up to the age of two and a half. At the time her mother went into hospital to have a second baby, her father too was in hospital with pneumonia. An aunt took the bewildered girl into her house. She was longing for her parents and desperately unhappy. Playing in the garden with a stick, she cut off the heads of all the flowers. When she saw her aunt appearing on the front steps she rushed in terror out of the gate, was run over by a car, badly hurt and admitted to hospital in great pain. Neither her mother nor her father could visit her. She had forgotten this experience until the birth of her second child, who for her became the little sister who had seemed to bring all the disaster.

Such memories or fantasies become all the more powerful if husband and wife have shared similár experiences. A couple who consciously very much wanted a second child were unable to have one, although no physical cause could be found which might have prevented conception. It emerged that the wife had lost a baby sister in infancy, and the husband a baby brother at birth. Both were brought up as only children, had experienced three-person relationships but found it difficult to contemplate a foursome family. All these inhibitions had remained unconscious; once the couple became aware of them and could face them consciously, the wife conceived, and they became a well-functioning foursome family.

People often express their fear that nothing will change, that the painful experiences of the past will inevitably be repeated. In fact the more conscious these fears are, the smaller is the likelihood of compulsive repetitions. But there is always hope, for people do learn and grow. The experiences with the second baby are not the same as with the first; each new baby is an unique individual and does not have to be a replica of a rival baby of the past, however painful the memories associated with it.

The birth of a girl after several boys or of a boy after several girls may raise special feelings of joy in the parents and special envy in the siblings whose success or failure to adjust to the new baby will largely depend on the attitude of the parents. The degree to which the parents themselves have coped with rivalries and jealousies will help their children not to become too frightened by similar—even murderous—feelings. The more the older children dare to show their ambivalence and have their hostile feelings understood, the greater the hope that they will be able to hold these feelings together with the love and delight which they also feel towards the new brother or sister.

The place which a new baby is allotted by the siblings becomes a most important part of his endowment for life. Although it is accidental whether a baby is the eldest or youngest, the big sister or the little brother, the role each has in his childhood family will remain with him for the rest of his life, and will affect all his future relationships. How this is enacted for better or worse depends largely on the interactions set up between the parents and the siblings, and on the parents' sensitivity and capacity to modify where necessary the patterns which develop. The siblings' love and admiration, or resentment and envy, fundamentally affect each child. The bossy elder sister whose photo the younger siblings proudly show round at school and who becomes a major attraction to their peers, is likely to use her bossiness throughout life in a benevolent and loving way. The spoiled little brother whose paintings decorate the older siblings' rooms and who curls up in their beds whenever they or he feel lonely is likely to use his charm and gifts with affection for the benefit of others. In short the acceptance and love of siblings can transform negative characteristics into positive ones. Each new baby's feelings of belonging will depend much on the way in which the family make room for him.

One of the most important relationships is that between grandchildren and grandparents. It can at its best be one which gives sheer joy without the tensions which are an inevitable part of the parent-child relationship. Married sons and daughters who are aware of these tensions and feel guilty about them may use their children, their parents' grandchildren, to give their own parents pleasure which they themselves felt unable to give. Equally, parents whose unrealistic expectations prevented them from straightforwardly loving their own children may greet the arrival of grandchildren with relief and delight as a new opportunity to express their love, and for a widowed grandparent, grandchildren are often the greatest comfort and help and can give new meaning to life.

Another aspect of the grandchildrens' importance is that they give their grandparents an assurance of the continuation of life. Grandparents suffering from a terminal illness have been known to linger on until they get the news of the birth of a grandchild, especially the first grandchild, and then are able to die knowing that life goes on. The consolation and solace which the dying obtain from the perpetuation of their own self in their offspring has been often described, 'Then death is successfully denied because the destruction of the old person is invalidated by the existence of the offspring.'[34]

The frequent coincidence of birth and death dates in families may result in the myth of 'one life for another'. The guilt and distress about a parent's death may then result in such a difficult confinement that the baby is stillborn or damaged.

Such date coincidence may also conjure up fantasies about reincarnation. A woman whose mother died the day before she gave birth to a baby girl, not only gave the baby her mother's first name, but felt she had been reborn in the child. She projected her mother's image on to this girl throughout her childhood, depriving her of her identity and leading to an unrealistic relationship between mother and daughter. In spite of the emphasis in our time on small isolated family units, grandparents, even after their death are of great importance to most families, and because we are attempting to remain in touch with family development in three generations we shall talk about grandparents in various contexts and in several chapters.

Feelings which had to be repressed in relation to a son or daughter because they were felt to be too disruptive, can often be freely expressed towards a grandchild or towards a great niece or nephew. The whole family circle may gain new interest and closeness through these children; expectations which had remained unfulfilled may be projected on to them. This process is often carried on by means of the names the children are given. Also some physical feature in the newborn may stamp him or her with an image which the child often surprisingly fulfils. Grandma's remark, 'He has exactly Uncle Joe's ears' may set the scene for the boy to become a replica of Uncle Joe.

Even adopted children may be given roles in the family by their adoptive parents which may meet the family needs rather than those of the child.

Yet children, even small babies, are not just screens for projections. They have their own unique personalities and are able to accept or reject alleged likenesses or the place assigned to them in the family, often without becoming aware of the part they are playing in this process. In the following chapters we shall try to show how the children and their family develop in mutual interaction.

4. The child becomes a person: pre-oedipal and oedipal phases

This chapter describes the enormous changes both in the child, who has ceased to be a brand new baby, and in the family as a whole during the first five years of the child's life. The child at this time is described as going through the pre-oedipal and oedipal phases.[35] At first—in the pre-oedipal period—the child's development takes place chiefly within the relationship with the mother. Many tasks have to be met and crises survived in this twosome relationship. The intense preoccupation of the mother and baby with each other docs not, of course, preclude either of them from engaging with other family members. We think, however, that these tasks and crises of the mother and child twosome are of primary importance at this stage, since they have to be more or less satisfactorily gone through if the baby is to move into and make the later psychological developments. The oedipal phase is essentially a threesome situation. The way a child achieves the move from the two person to three person situation has enormous bearing on the evolution of his individual personality. The capacity of a family to enable a child to move from the twosome with the mother to the threesome with mother and father, and the manner, style and qualities of family life at the time, we believe to be chiefly determined by two important factors: the parents' own experiences of moving through the same phase in their own childhood, and the nature of their marital relationship.

The whole oedipal phase is one in which parents and children find themselves passionately involved, and is, in our view, therefore, one that brings the child and parents near to having incestuous feelings. The issue of incest is in many ways the central theme of the whole book, as incestuous wishes produce such intensely felt and momentous secrets.

The tasks to be met by the child in the pre-oedipal phase can be summarized briefly:

1 He has to be able to establish within himself sources of basic

trust[36] and optimism. These come from the regularity and predict-ability with which his needs have been met from the beginning.

2   He needs to have experienced an appropriate balance between gratification and frustration of his needs. The needs of a baby must be met reasonably promptly so that too much despair and panic are avoided. This enables the baby to develop some capacity to care for himself without having prematurely developed attempts at independence forced upon him.

3   The baby begins to become capable of loving, and so to a small extent, of trying to care for others. He becomes capable of appreci-ating that other people do exist, and have certain needs like his own.

4   From the second year onwards the sources of self-esteem and security that the child should have gained within himself are being threatened by his incipient awareness of his own capacity to hurt and hate. He begins to realize that these capacities could alienate him from those he loves.

5   He likes to control his mother, but, having a belief in his own omnipotence, goes through times when he believes he may make himself feared and hated by the exercise of his fantasized power.

6   As a toddler he begins to worry that increasing physical indepen-dence might result in desertion and loss of his mother.

7   Gradually, in continuing to experience love and appreciation although aware of his increased assertiveness, he becomes less disturbed by anxiety about the harm he is capable of doing and he begins to clothe the self in more and more individual characteristics.

8   There are many particular qualities of character which establish the child as a personality in his own right but if he has developed the general qualities of confidence and trust he can also begin to have an increasingly definite sexual, (more properly 'gender'), identity. The child's sexual arousal and curiosity has its impact on the next move, that is to say the move into the oedipus complex of feelings and fantasies.

All these points are connected with tasks and conflicts with implications for his developing sense of security and their outcome inevitably influences subsequent emotional and family relationships. This in part comes about because the child is left with a host of fantasies within himself. They form a store of 'family secrets' which in adulthood he will attempt to re-enact with a new family. Secret beliefs in the cruelty and hostility of the world may come from bad experiences in these earliest years, whilst from good experiences come optimism, whether unconscious or overt, and a belief in the bounteousness of life and nature. A belief in the incompatability of loving and hating feelings (most likely to come from being cared for by those who themselves had not been able to find a way to cope with their own mixed feelings) can be fed by difficulties in the second year of life. At that time sadism and masochism can become important secret longings or fears, and may eventually find their way, as we have said, into marital relationships, where both partners have grown up with the same underlying secret convictions, and engage in a mutually cruel and hurtful form of emotional bond. Particular conditions or qualifications upon parental love and care may result in children developing correspondingly slanted beliefs about which aspects of themselves are lovable and worthwhile. These beliefs will affect their internal sources of feelings of self-approval and esteem as they develop. Aspects of such preconceptions about the conditions and determinants of parental love will form 'secrets', whose influences we will be attempting to demonstrate in stories from people's lives.

Examples from the lives of 'normal' pre-school children show them going through the pre-oedipal and oedipal stages. *Frederick* was a well behaved and sturdy twenty-month-old boy, who had began to be able to walk sensibly enough. One day when feeding the ducks in the park lake, he ran off suddenly and tripped over, falling into the lake. Just there the water was deep and he sank out of his depth. His mother immediately pulled him out and he was perfectly all right, but cold and frightened. At home, that evening, his mother reminded him to tell his father of his fright and he said 'Freddie fell in the water.' The next day, whilst out shopping with his mother he suddenly ran into the road, and she had to grab him quickly back. But this time it was obviously no accident. He seemed to have tried out his mother's reflexes deliberately, and he did not again do anything similarly dangerous. This ordinary little boy, with the developing independence of the toddler phase was learning of the possibility of separateness from mother, and testing out the security of her care, within his new realization of freedom.

At times there is interaction between child and parents as the child goes through the oedipal phase.

A conversation between *Sarah*, aged four, and her mother, began by Sarah saying, 'I love you so much, Mummy, I want to marry you. . . . No, that isn't any good because you can't give me any babies. Daddy could give me a baby. I think I'll ask him. . . . No you wouldn't like that . . . so perhaps you had better ask him. Could you ask him to put a baby-seed in my tummy?' Mother said, 'No, when you grow up you can have a Daddy of your own to give you a baby,' and Sarah replied, 'Yes, people don't like sharing their Daddies, do they? They like a special one just for them. But you see I want a baby right now.' Mother answered, 'But you're too little now to look after a baby and to feed it . . . besides you're my baby at the moment.' Sarah ended the conversation by replying, 'I know—but I could feed it—not with bosoms but with bottles— and then I wouldn't need a bottle any more.' Sarah has begun to understand quite well about growing up, about sexual physical differences and about the different roles in parenthood of the two sexes. She is wondering about her own future but can still only imagine it as being mainly bound up with her parents. Her mother is trying to give sensible enlightenment whilst keeping her daughter's vulnerability in mind.

From this picture of a child working out her relationship with her mother and father and attempting to reconcile some of the problems brought by her joint love of them and need for them, we can imagine how a number of wishes and daydreams are formed and are partly remembered and partly absorbed into the child's repertoire of unconscious fantasies. It is this tangled and bewildering mixture of love, hate, jealousies, rivalries, sexual wishes, fears and expectations stemming from the oedipal time that is the most fecund source of 'secrets' in our sense of the word. These secrets will be found to underlie adult choice of marital partner and to shape many of the attitudes towards the children that result from that union. Children's loyalty and accuracy of response to such secrets in their parents' minds is to us one of the most striking features of family life. One of our main purposes throughout this book is to show how a person's later life can be influenced by the long-term effects of happenings in these early times of life.

Sheila's case shows how difficulties in the pre-oedipal and oedipal phase may threaten successful development in adolescence. She was sent to see a child psychiatrist because she had lost twenty pounds in weight in the preceding fourteen months. She was thirteen and a half years old and had menstruated once when she was twelve and a quarter. Her fearfulness at the thought that she might put on weight, her compulsive commitment to physical exercises, and the constant wrangles with her mother over eating and sustenance were all characteristic of anorexia nervosa. She was the youngest of three daughters and had no brother. Her sisters, twenty-six and twenty-four years old, were both married and living far from their parents, one in the United States and the other in the North of England. They were never seen in the course of the family treatment undertaken on account of Sheila's condition. Father, *Mr Knight*, was fifty-three. He had a technical job of some responsibility in local government, which he took extremely seriously. His early life had been impoverished, for his parents had suffered financial hardship during the economic depression of the pre-war years. His father had been out of work for long periods, as his craft had almost disappeared. However the family with its three sons had stayed together and he had no recollection of substantial unhappiness. There was some mystery about the origins of Mr Knight's parents, for they had both been silent and uncommunicative people. Mr Knight had had to leave school at the age of fourteen in order to work to help the family, and he had not been able to get further training until after war service.

Mrs Knight had had a similar background in an inner London area but her family had been much poorer, for her father's unemployment was complicated firstly by his drunkenness and later by pulmonary tuberculosis. When he became physically enfeebled, Mrs Knight had nursed him lovingly, but when she was eighteen he died. His tiny appetite and the wasting away of his flesh was brought to Mrs Knight's mind by Sheila's similarly small appetite, and her skinniness once her compulsive undereating had become established.

Sheila had always been thought by her parents to be a resourceful, imaginative and rather wilful person. One particular anecdote had stuck in Mr and Mrs Knight's mind's about Sheila's early life; at the age of four, she had had a row with her mother and had gone to a neighbour saying that her mother had abandoned her. This was thought by the parents to be characteristic of a tendency of their youngest daughter to overdramatize, but, in their view, it was also expressive of the intensity of her dependence on her mother.

When they all first came to see us, the family atmosphere was dominated by the rows between mother and daughter about eating. Mrs Knight would rage and despair over whether Sheila had eaten half a piece of thinly sliced bread at breakfast or whether it had been a whole slice. At the same time Sheila would attempt to bargain her food intake for parental permission to get up early and go on 'training' runs. There were also intense quarrels with her mother over more usual adolescent issues such as the extent to which she should conform to school uniform requirements, how many times a week she should go out in the evening and whether or not she could stay at home on her own when her parents went away at the weekend. When the family rows were recounted in the interviews with the whole family, father's rather lofty attitude to the difficulties became very apparent. From time to time Mrs Knight attempted to elicit her husband's support for the stands that she wished to take about Sheila, but on each occasion he would evade the issue by his abstract approach or by outright refusal to state his opinion or to be forced into taking sides.

Over some months the following themes became clear. Firstly, the rows about food had produced a very childish situation for Sheila. Her whole life was watched over very carefully by her mother. What time she got up in the morning, how she had slept, what was happening to her bowels and her weight, how the weather might affect her, and her capacity to take part in activities, were all endlessly discussed by her mother; and there were the constant rows about food. Sheila, although apparently trying to get more freedom for herself from her mother's restrictions and concerns, was by her self-starvation ensuring that her mother had to be intensely involved with every aspect of her body-function as though she were a much younger child. The rows with her mother gave the impression that she resented every bit of parental control, but her passion to lose weight continued to ensure detailed parental surveillance. Secondly, the pattern of the family alliances became quite clear. The family as a whole never seemed to be able to agree about anything. Although mother and daughter were ostensibly locked in the rows, mother was furious with her husband and daughter to the extent that at the time of the first interview she was planning to get a flat on her own in order 'to leave them to it together'. She felt that her daughter and husband had united together to make her out to be stupid, ignorant and boring. Father and daughter spent much time together out of mother's earshot, talking seriously and intently. Father denied that there could be any reason for his wife to believe that he sided with Sheila against her, but in the joint interviews it was clear that there was a flirtatious aspect of Sheila's behaviour towards her father, which pleased and even captivated him. In fact Sheila was a very beautiful, slim and elegant girl, whilst her mother was fat and often anxious and flustered. Despite the terrible upsets, Sheila could usually remain poised and quick witted.

During their joint therapy we were able to arrive at an understanding of the family's interaction and its origin that took the following form. There was evident persistency and re-creation of early childhood issues between Sheila and her mother, (pre-oedipal derivatives or fixations). In earlier childhood Sheila had experienced her mother's care as somewhat begrudged. Indeed the mother had not wanted to have a third daughter, and she had always found her difficult to please and a contrast to her easy and pleasurable older children. She had had episodes of depression throughout Sheila's life and she had felt that Sheila's dependence had delayed her employment out of the home, something which she had longed for. For us, Sheila's childhood complaint to the neighbour fitted into this picture convincingly. Sheila, at the time the family came to see us, showed herself to be very feminine but at the same time seemed very anxious about her imminent womanhood and knew quite well that in some of her wishes she had wanted to be her father's son. In the threesome that was left by the older daughters' marriages it was rare for any family events to be shared wholeheartedly by all three members. Indeed it was the pattern for the mother and daughter to be together, commonly in conflict; for father and daughter to be together, in discussion and alliance; or for mother and father to be together, but usually only in bed. Mrs Knight would have liked to have more of her husband's waking company, but she felt she was not respected by him and was no longer attractive to him.

It was clear that for Mrs Knight there was in her care for her daughter during her 'illness' a re-creation of her sad closeness to her own father in his last years. The distance she had come to feel between herself and her husband also re-created for her some of the qualities she had experienced many times in her childhood when she had felt that her father was alienated from his family and unavailable to her. For Mr Knight, his daughter reminded him of his wife when she had been young and just out of girlhood. He had greatly enjoyed the closeness with her as a young woman, for her openness and expressiveness had been of particular importance to him in their courtship. It had seemed such a welcome contrast and relief from the taciturn style of his parents. Later in the work with the family it helped Mrs Knight considerably when Mr Knight was able to tell her this. Her warm expressiveness had seemed a fulfilment of his childhood wishes that his mother would comfort him more openly and talk to him. He had enjoyed his children very much and knew that now that her sisters had left home he was concentrating what before had been divided into three on to Sheila.

We can see how for both Mr and Mrs Knight their experience of their parents in childhood shaped what endured in their persisting oedipal fantasies and so affected their choice of marital partners and their expectations. Mr Knight in recalling those aspects of his mother that he enjoyed, hoped for fulfilment of such enjoyments with his wife. In remembering what he had wanted of his mother he was also, in some ways, remembering aspects of being a father by partially modelling himself on his father. But it also seemed that in his closeness and ability to have friendship with his daughter he was also drawing on aspects of himself that had been modelled on his mother. His wife had unconsciously recognized some such capacities, and had expected, rightly, that his tender ability to identify with his mother would enable him to be close to her and sympathetic to her needs for care and gentle love. Similarly, Mrs Knight in having been close to her father in his last years had learned not only something of what she wanted and feared in men but also something of the needs of men for a certain sort of vigorous comradely ('masculine') company which, initially, she had been able to give and which had strengthened the marriage. Later, she had felt that her daughters in their intellectual abilities had surpassed her and she ceased to believe in her ability to meet her husband's needs for such company and stimulation. However her daughters had been able to learn from her that it is possible to have a definite femininity whilst also having male attributes.

In general the way both partners of the marriage can express something of both genders, helps toddlers realize that developing into a boy or a girl does not have to cut them off completely from everything of the other sex. The parents' ways of being their own sex, their happiness, contentment or disappointment in their sex and its possibilities are observed by the young child as he or she begins to become aware of being a boy or a girl (a realization that is well to the fore already by the third year of life). This is another example of the many ways that the little child has to integrate and balance the opposing possibilities and choices he has between dependence and independence, agreeing and opposing, loving and hating. The integration of opposites into qualities of individuality is well under way in the third year of life, but they are never totally resolved by the child's coming down completely on to one side or the other. Much of the tumultuousness of the little child's feelings comes from the oscillations around such opposites, which can be very rapid. These first attempts in the toddler to form a balanced personality are usually most intensely worked out with one person at a time, but the case of the Knight family illustrates how one parent (or indeed both parents) can demonstrate both opposing aspects (masculine and feminine) within one personality. Unresolved oedipal aspects of Mrs Knight's development had influenced Sheila's pre-oedipal development by allowing her to develop both feminine and masculine aspects, and to avoid the task of establishing for herself a coherent, unitary gender identity as a basis for learning to relate jointly with both parents: the major task of the oedipal phase.

The intensity of Sheila's oedipal phase and her imperative need to have her parents only one at a time was brought out during treatment. We arrived at a point when it seemed important to tell Sheila that there had been a time in her life when she had very much wanted to have her father to herself and to get rid of her mother. She denied this vigorously, as we had expected, (for very few adolescents are consciously aware of this desire, common though it is). Her mother, however, was surprised by the denial and turned to her daughter saying, 'Don't you remember, when you were four, you often came into bed with your father and me. You used to lie between us and dig your elbow into my ribs and say "Now you can go." ' The persistence of these oedipal longings and their reappearance in her adolescent pairing with father against mother, was clear.

In Sheila's crisis in early adolescence unresolved aspects of her earlier childhood can be perceived. Some of the feeding battles we would see as having direct ancestry in baby battles over feeding and control of baby habits. These aspects persisted because of happenings in earlier years consequent upon her family position, her mother's state of mind and attitudes to her and the state of her marriage. In adolescence, as we shall be discussing later, there is a revival of many pre-oedipal and oedipal feelings. Sheila went back to a demanding, controlling and close, albeit exceedingly ambivalent relationship to her mother. Mrs Knight found herself having to care for Sheila as if she once again were a baby. In part this filled a need for Mrs Knight who was suffering from the feeling that her husband was distant from her. At the same time Sheila, once she had secured her mother's full commitment by the infantilism that her self-starvation produced, could indulge fully her longings to outshine her mother in making bright conversation with which to captivate and monopolize her father. This showed that her persisting oedipal wish was not to find a substitute for her father, (the normal developmental use of surviving oedipal fantasies, leading ultimately to the foundation of a new family), but to have her actual father to herself, in competition with her mother. In other words she had not resolved her oedipal longings, but she simply wished to make them safe. This she did by exaggerating her obvious need for her mother's detailed care.

For Freud and many psychoanalysts of today, the stage of the oedipal complex is perhaps the most crucial in its consequences for mental health and personality structure. Freud saw it as a time through which no one passed without encountering difficulties and anxieties. From our long contact with married couples and families we believe that this view of the importance of the oedipal phase is, if anything, understated. We see it as a time when personal disturbance and neurosis may indeed arise, but also as a period of life and psychological growth which is essential for the development of the capacity to love and eventually to marry and participate in the creation of a new family. It is also clear that although we are fully aware of the stresses and challenges facing the family in the modern world we retain constant awareness of the irreplaceable importance of the family in nurturing the qualities of caring and the capacity for loving that people value in each other.

We think that the oedipal time of child development is of central importance if we are to understand the marriages and family stories we are describing here. Freud's[37] first thoughts about the origins of neurosis led him to emphasize the role of the external trauma and especially of the trauma of sexual seduction in childhood and adolescence. But as his work continued, he began to feel surprised at the frequency with which he could discern the evidence of such sexual seductions in his patients' accounts of their lives. Eventually he came to the conclusion that he had been mistaken in accepting his patients' experiences as representing actual happenings in their early lives. What he had initially taken to be the derivatives of such traumas in his patients he came to believe to be the outcome of secretly and disguisedly expressed socially forbidden sexual longings present in them as young children. He came to understand that many of the supposed sexual events had not really occurred at all, but were the outcome of the child's longings for possession of the parents and of the fear and rivalries that such longings aroused. Freud had noted that the pre-school child had already a history of sexuality (which is what Freud called the sensual aspects of the baby's oral, anal and genital pleasures) but that it was not until the fifth to sixth year that that sexuality involved the child in actually wanting its sexual needs met by some sort of response from another person. When the child is reaching the stage of participation in three person relationships, as we have discussed above, when intense physical longing for exclusive possession of the loved parent is combined with the child's knowledge of its capacity to hate and wish destruction, then the full oedipal situation is possible. Essentially, the child in longing to have its parent to itself has to wonder about eliminating the rival adult, the parent of the same sex. However, as Freud was the first to point out, the child has longings for exclusive rights to both parents. The problem is not just that the child wishes to get rid of the parent of the same sex, but that the child also wishes to have the same-sex parent to himself as much as he wants the opposite-sex parent. Of course it is the child's feelings for the opposite-sex parent that are most likely to become the starting point for his adult sexual life.

Although the oedipal situation is a fertile source of conflicts and tangles for the developing personality, we see it also as an essential trial ground on which will develop the child's capacity to have intense loving relationships. These do not have to be exclusive, and can therefore be widened to take in other children and adults in the family, and later in the outside world. Further, we differ from Freud in seeing the parents' role as not only passive and punitive, or traumatic and seductive—the possibilities most readily noted by Freud and most subsequent psychoanalysts. We see the child as needing, in addition, the parents' responsive love in the oedipal phase to form the basis of the ability he will have when grown up to give and receive love, both physically and emotionally. The little girl needs to know that her father is a bit in love with her, (just as the adolescent girl whose father feels absolutely no erotic interest in her cannot believe that anyone else could love her). This does not gainsay the need of the five-year-old girl being loved by her mother also. But the little girl needs also to believe that her mother takes her seriously as a rival for her father's affection. Only so can she take herself and her own life seriously too. Similarly the little boy can love and adore his father throughout the oedipal phase, but he needs to know as well that his mother is proud and excited by his masculinity and that his longing to be preferred to his father by his mother is not totally ridiculous. Again, in adolescence, a boy has to feel that the gleam in his mother's eye at his growing adult body is not solely maternal.

Because this situation includes such an intensity of feelings from both parent and child, it is not at all surprising, in our view, that the oedipal experience is so often associated with incestuous qualities. We hope we have made it clear that we think that healthy development of the capacity to love and to make a family, depends on feelings being permitted to exist in the family of a sort that in principle might result in incest. That does not mean to say that we view incest as an actual physical event between parents and children as in any way appropriate or acceptable. It does mean that fantasies of incest are almost invariably present both in the child's mind and in the parent's mind.

People who have never negotiated the oedipal phase, whose development stopped or was distorted while still at the stage of the exclusive two person relationship, present social problems. *Mr Green*, a man of forty-five, came to see us immediately after his discharge from prison, having served a year's sentence for committing incest with his thirteen-year-old daughter. He was completely bewildered and uncomprehending. He had never made a secret of his love for his daughter, and his wife never objected to it. But at some point she spoke about it to a neighbour, the neighbour mentioned it to a welfare officer, and the welfare officer brought in the police. Mr Green insisted that he had done no harm to *Anne*, she was beautiful, healthy and clever—she had flourished through his love. When we suggested to him that there are different ways to express a father's love for his daughter, he put his hand into his pocket and took out a charming old-fashioned medallion with a woman's portrait. He was asked: 'Is that Anne?' 'No', he said, 'That is my mother.' He then said that he was two years old when his mother died and as his father could not look after him, he was adopted by his mother's younger sister. He had a very good home there, was fond of his aunt and she of him, but 'Of course, I could never love her as I would have loved my mother.' His wife and her family were neighbours. They grew up together like brother and sister. She was very attached to her father, and he liked him too. They married young and were very happy together, but he was sure that he never felt for his wife as he would have felt for his mother. But when Anne was born, he felt that she was the reincarnation of his mother, and he could love her as he would have loved his mother. When asked whether he would have wanted to have such a close physical relationship with his mother, he looked sad and said: 'You see, I never had it.' Having been taken over by a loving aunt and offered a good home, he may have been little aware of his loss at the time his mother died. His aunt probably did all she could to make him forget it, and there could be no mourning, and no opportunity to live through and progress from his need for his mother's exclusive care and love.

When he now came home from prison, his wife made him very welcome. She was happy to have him back again—but Anne was in a boarding school, and Mr Green said, 'I feel as if I had lost my mother all over again.' At this point his therapist tried to say something about the adult's need to tolerate loss and separation, wondering whether he could in the present situation work through some of the grief which he himself linked so closely with the original loss, when he was deprived of his mother. But he refused to talk any more. He had only come to consult someone because he had hoped they might be able to do something to bring Anne home again; if that was impossible, he needed no other help; he had survived his mother's loss and he would survive this one. When the therapist suggested it might be helpful for him to come with his wife so that they both could understand better why she had been unable to replace his mother in his life, he said firmly but politely that his wife would never dream of coming; she was quite content with things as they were. It seems that he neither wanted nor could use our help to deal with the limitations of his relationships. We concluded that this man, who lost his mother in the early formative years before he reached the oedipal phase, had developed what we think corresponds to Michael Balint's idea of 'the basic fault', a kind of deficiency-state in which only two objects exist: the individual and his primary object: his mother. According to Balint[38] such people cannot be reached through ordinary adult language; they must be allowed to regress.

'The patient must be allowed to regress either to the setting, that is, to the particular form of object relationship which caused the original deficiency state, or even to some stage before it. This is a precondition which must be fulfilled before the patient can give up, very tentatively at first, his compulsive pattern. Only after that can the patient 'begin anew', that is develop new patterns of object relationship to replace those given up. These new patterns will be less defensive and thus more flexible, offering him more possibility to adapt himself to reality under less tension and friction than hitherto.'

This Mr Green did not want to do.

Problems about the expression of widespread—indeed universal incestuous longings springing from the oedipal phase are extremely common. We see all families having to face these issues, in the child and in the adult members, and we think that although they are never 'resolved' in the sense of being eliminated, the conflicts of these times leave their mark on subsequent human relationships. All parents, in facing the feelings in their children, experience an awakening of their own oedipal feelings. We shall illustrate this with another example:

Mrs Peters complained bitterly that when her husband came home from work, instead of greeting her, he went straight upstairs into their three-year-old daughter's bedroom and stood for a long time 'adoringly' by her bed. Mrs Peters felt angry and rejected and had tried to tell her husband about her feelings, but he had been quite unable to understand her and had responded by getting angry himself.

In talking about her anxiety that her husband cared more for the little girl than for her, she began to remember how often her own mother had interrupted a flirtatious game between her, (an only child), and her father. She recalled her feelings of triumph and guilt on occasions when she felt that her father loved her more than her mother, and how much her mother resented their close relationship. After speaking about these childhood memories, she reported with much emotion a dream: she was lying in bed, asleep, and dreamed that she woke with a shock because her father (who had died before she married) was in the room, walking round and round her bed, looking at her very seductively. When Mrs Peters was able to tell her husband about this dream, he too began to recall childhood memories. He had never known his father, who died during the war before he, a first child, was born. His mother cherished her husband's memory in her little boy, who became her sole comfort and close companion. During his adolescence he became worried about the close tie with his mother, and when he married he made a conscious effort to loosen it by moving away to a foreign land. He and his wife had much in common and were very happy to begin with. But his little daughter's seductive infatuation for her Daddy had stirred up some of the feelings which he, at her age, had had for his mother—just as they had stirred up in his wife her feelings for her father.

By sharing their experience, Mr and Mrs Peters understood the great importance of this phase in their daughter's and in their own life. They became aware that the beloved parent can only renounce the desirable loved child with a sense of loss.[39]

We hoped that Mr and Mrs Peters' understanding of their own feelings and their ability to share this understanding, would free their young daughter to use her oedipal experience as a growing point for her life and for her femininity. If they had continued to express their anxieties in angry or seductive behaviour towards her, she might have found it difficult to reach a comfortable resolution of the problems.

Intense family bonds of love and caring spring from passionate feelings which must inevitably carry the possibility of forbidden wishes for physical closeness. Children find that from the beginning they receive and are enabled and encouraged to give their most intense and often exclusive love first to their parents and later to their siblings. It is therefore natural that, when children come to wish for physical expression of their love and when they experience the first stirrings of their own sexuality, these feelings should be directed towards those to whom they have always been devoted in love and admiration. And yet, of course, children must also learn that their intense wishes must eventually move them out of the family circle. The parents' need to be parents is, as Benedek has said, a definite stage in the development of adulthood, but the expression of this need is coloured by unconscious wishes to re-enact experiences from their own childhood, including sensual enjoyment of bodily contact with their own parents. The family is the place in which the parents, as sexual adults, experience their own sexual pleasure and excitement, and this creates an atmosphere in which the children's own sexual longings are intensified.

Sensuality in the family has three components. There is the sex life of the parents; the children's developing sensual longings; and the parents' tendency to re-experience their own childhood sensuality in the relationship with their children.

It is therefore inevitable that incestuous fantasies are part of the secret life of every family.[40] For children to develop into healthy, loving and sexual adults, these fantasies are necessary, but their overt expression has to be controlled by the parents. The parents' ability to achieve this in their physical contact with their small children is 'internalized' by the children as they grow up, so that they can contain their incestuous longings for their parents during adolescence, when these sensuous feelings are heightened by bio-logical changes. And this, in turn, will help them, when they are parents, to express physical love for their children, without endan-gering them by sexual seduction.

We have observed with many others that actual enactment of sexuality between parent and child is most common in families where there is a lack of sexual fulfilment in the marital relationship and where contact with the child is a displacement substitute for marital loving. The parent who has suffered in early childhood from deprivation of love and care is more likely to find himself incapable of withstanding the longing to express his sexual frustra-tion in physical contact with his child. Similarly children respond more often to the temptation to resort to sexual expression of their feelings when they have disappointments and loss in their early and current life.

The most frequent overt expression of incestuous feelings and fantasies is probably among siblings. The young child's intense curiosity about bodies can lead to exciting play and thus become highly sexualized. Within the family this is often tolerated, and less productive of anxiety-making secrets than a similar relationship between a parent and a child. Yet everybody working with family-relationships, in particular marriages, knows how strongly these later adult relationships are affected by the previous erotic relationships between brothers and sisters.

Monica was nineteen when she married *Fred*, her brother *John*'s best friend. Throughout childhood and adolescence John and Monica had been inseparable, and it was probably because this extreme closeness began to worry John that he promoted his sister's marriage to Fred. He was best man at the wedding, became the regular Sunday-dinner guest of the young couple and a valued companion on their holidays. They were a happy triangle, until, eight months after the wedding, John was killed in a car crash. Monica was inconsolable. From the moment of John's death she turned away from Fred, whose patient attempts to win her back failed. She treated him like a stranger and also took no interest in her baby daughter, born two months after John's death. She deteriorated in health and after she had had to be admitted to a mental hospital, she refused to return to her husband and child.

When the little girl was five years old, the husband started divorce proceedings with which Monica eagerly co-operated, although she refused his request for custody of the child. She promised to return home and to her child as soon as the divorce was through and Fred had left. When she returned she appeared to be completely changed, and became a loving and caring mother. She reverted to her maiden name, recovered her previous health and vitality, and was successful not only as a housewife and mother but also in her professional job. She refused to see Fred, or to have any direct contact with him, although she allowed him access to the child. To us it seems that in marrying Fred, Monica felt on an unconscious level that she was marrying John. When John died, Fred was dead for her too, and being married to him became a lie, against which she rebelled. Perhaps Fred's extraordinary co-operativeness throughout all phases of the marriage may indicate a tacit collusion from the beginning with Monica's and probably John's way of perceiving the relationship between all three.

Often when a young man marries his sister's best friend, (sometimes the sister has the same Christian name), or a girl marries her brother's best friend, severe marriage problems may result, as we have seen in the example of Mr and Mrs Cant in Chapter 2.

But the child's relationship with a parent normally predates that with a sibling, and incestuous feelings between parent and child, accordingly, are evidently stronger and more basic (and more socially abhorred) than sibling incest. Often it seems that the incestuous fantasies between brother and sister can be seen as a diversion from the daughter's feelings for her father, which are considered more disruptive to the stability of the family. It also seems that father-daughter incest is more frequent (or more freely acknowledged) than mother-son incest.

'If mother-son incest occurs as often as father-daughter incest we certainly do not hear about it; yet in our society there seems to be less prohibition against expression of partially seductive attitudes of mother towards son than against father towards daughter. This strict genital taboo may allow for greater expression of partial (polymorphous) sexual indulgence. The loosening to this extent of the incest barrier nevertheless produces its own pathological process in the genesis of sexual perversions.'[41]

C. G. Jung[42] in his writings on the mystical and symbolic aspects of mother-son incest, comments on the son's longing for his mother, and his fears of her, not so much in terms of sexual incest but as fantasies about re-entry into the mother, a return to the womb. We have often been impressed by the extent to which the man's incestuous wishes for his mother are coloured by the fear that she wishes to deprive him of his masculinity—a fear expressed in fantasies of castration.

Some of the implications of incest for the family group are illustrated by the case of the *Brown family*. This consisted of the father, aged forty-six, the mother thirty, *Susan* eleven, twin girls eight, and two boys, five and two. Only the boys were of the marriage. Susan was the mother's child by her first husband and the twins were illegitimate. Mr Brown was charged with indecently assaulting Susan, after the mother had told neighbours of frequent incidents of intensive petting and mutual masturbation with the child which she had partly observed herself and partly dragged out of Susan. The neighbours informed the police and Mr Brown was arrested when he came home from work. His wife was beside herself with distress. She had never anticipated this, but just thought he would be told off. She was in such a state of shock that the police asked a woman probation officer to visit her.

The husband was remanded to prison for a month while waiting for medical and psychiatric reports. The first suggestion was that Susan and the twin girls should be taken into care. However, largely because of the probation officer's reports and her skilled handling of the case the husband was discharged after one month with a three-year probation order to work with a male officer. All the children stayed in the parental home, and the female probation officer who had visited the mother while the father was in prison continued to work with Mrs Brown and Susan, also for three years. She had from the beginning helped the mother to look at her own involvement in the situation, and had not accepted the general view of the case, shared by the police, that the mother, small and childlike in appearance, was exploited by a brutal, dominant, controlling husband.

With the mother's help the following story emerged:

Mrs Brown was an only child with a ne'er do well father who was very attractive, especially to women, and quite irresponsible. When she was in her early teens, he gambled the home away and went to live with another woman. He completely disappeared from her life, and never made any attempt to see her or support her, but yet she never forgave her mother for not having been able to keep her adored father at home.

When she was sixteen, her mother died quite suddenly of a heart attack in her arms, leaving her with an acute sense of guilt for having been so hostile and angry with her.

The widowed mother of her boyfriend offered her a home, and became a much loved substitute mother. When the girl was eighteen the young couple married—the young husband reminded her of her own father. After a year Susan was born, and about six months later the young husband disappeared. He had gone off with another girl. His wife and Susan stayed on with his mother, who looked after the baby while the young woman went out to work. When Susan was eighteen months old her mother was pregnant again, this time by her employer, a married man, who was most attractive and very irresponsible. He refused to take any responsibility when twin girls were born, and the mother-in-law now had a big family to look after.

A lodger in the house, Mr Brown, a bachelor in his fortieth year, took a great interest in the charming and helpless young woman and her three little girls. He became especially fond of the twins, and when they were two years old the couple married and set up a home of their own. The new Mrs Brown was very grateful for all his help and support. He was so dependable, but she saw him as quite unattractive, adding that this was just as well as all attractive men seemed to leave her. Her picture of her new husband was quite different from the reality: he was actually a tall, good-looking man, always meticulously turned out and well-mannered. He never made any advances to her before they married, and she was very surprised that he wanted a sexual relationship at all. After their two boys were born she had refused further intercourse. The reason she gave was that she very easily became pregnant and did not want any more children.

Up to the time of Mr Brown's arrest, the family had presented a most stable picture. Mrs Brown was an excellent housewife and a caring mother. All the children were healthy and thriving. The three girls did well at school and showed no problems. Mr Brown had been very distressed by his wife's sexual refusal, ('It was she,' he complained, 'Who had made me into a man, and then she rejected me'), but accepted her decision and took a night job to ease matters. He provided well for the family, had adopted the twins and was a very good father to all the children. When the husband took his night job, his wife arranged for him to share a bedroom with Susan—after all, as he was hardly ever at home during the night, it was a waste of space for him to have a room of his own. Susan, a lovely and seductive little girl, the image of her mother, was very fond of her step-father and delighted with the plan, and her mother did everything possible to stimulate her husband's interest in Susan. It seemed that while she kept sexually away from him, she got vicarious satisfaction from the sex-play between father and daughter, identifying with Susan and thus providing herself with the fulfilment of one of her own earliest and strongest wishes —being fully loved by her father.

This became very clear when the skilled probation officer helped her to explore her feelings and motives. She spoke with great excitement about her husband's affectionate care for Susan and the flirtatious games they were playing. She got quite upset when she spoke of her husband's love for Susan's long fair hair, which he liked to brush for hours on end. When the probation officer asked what was so upsetting about this she started to cry, and then said that her mother would not let her father brush her hair. She had cut it off.

The probation officer's report about this family contributed to the decision to discharge Mr Brown after a month. By the time he returned home, his wife had become aware how much of her feelings for her father she had projected on to him. While she rejected him sexually because he was not like the idealized father, she nevertheless used him to re-enact with Susan her own incestuous fantasies in relation to her father. During his three years on probation with the male probation officer, Mr Brown also learned to understand something of why his own feelings for his mother had made him so receptive to his wife's projections. He had been one of many children with a violent and highly-sexed father and an always-pregnant mother whom he loved dearly and wanted to protect from his father's violence. But she rejected his protection and he was sent away to school. He kept away from women until he met his wife. Her helplessness and need of protection attracted him, and so did the fact that, like his mother, she became so easily pregnant. When she rejected him sexually, he was sad but accepted it without a murmur, because he expected to be rejected by women. When his probation officer helped him to feel that he had his own real value both as a husband and as a father, Mr Brown became more able to find his own proper place in the family, and could develop for the first time a belief in his right to have a wife and be a sexually adult man.

The female probation officer kept in touch with the mother and Susan. Susan was at the age when 'the remoulding of the infantile sex-life is also linked with the readiness of the child in puberty to transfer its reawakened erotic sexual needs and wishes to its parents.'[43] She was therefore an important and active member in the therapy for the family, which quite often met as a group with both probation officers.

Through this work the family were not only enabled to remain together but developed more stable and realistic relationships through their increased awareness of what had been going on between them. When Mrs Brown understood that her attitude to her husband included a fear of letting her husband give her what she wanted from her father, she could accept contraceptive measures. In the past she had refused them in order to have an excuse not to have a sexual relationship with her husband, which, she feared, would separate her from her cherished fantasies of her father.

Processes of unconscious collusive interaction in the family, involving incestuous fantasies, are illustrated by the Brown case. These processes are usually least recognized where there is a prosecution for incest. As a rule the father, (or, in the case of a mother-son incest, the mother), is charged with an individual offence, punished and removed from the family, whose involvement in what has happened is rarely explored. Yet it would be precisely such exploration of the family interactions which might set a healing and rehabilitating process in motion, as we have seen in the example of the Brown family. Our conviction is that incest is rarely only an individual's offence but is an expression of collusive interaction processes in the family, based on shared incestuous fantasies.

On some level, everybody working in the field of family problems knows this. Again and again we have heard from social workers or health visitors the puzzled question: 'Why did the mother not stop what was going on between father and daughter? She knew about it for years and almost seemed to have brought it about.' Perhaps one of the reasons why it is difficult to explore these questions is that even the mention of the word incest evokes feelings of panic and guilt.

We have stated our belief that incestuous feelings and fantasies within the family are universal, and play an important part in the healthy development of the child. Because they are so prevalent and so strong, society needs to maintain the age-old incest taboo as a defence against the threat of interbreeding which would endanger the human race (at a biological level) and the family (at a social level). These taboos are of biological and social value, but because of their primordial origin they arouse feelings of irrational disgust and horror, and are not accessible to rational understanding. Freud,[44] quoting the support of J. G. Frazer says: 'We are ignorant of the origin of the horror of incest and cannot even tell in what direction to look for it.' He also says: 'We are driven to believe that the rejection of evidence to show the extent to which creative writers centre round the theme of incest . . . is principally a product of the distaste which humans feel for their early wishes, now overtaken by repression.'

Because of the horror of incest feelings and fantasies they are almost always completely denied. Yet we have learned that cultural changes can bring about the easing of taboos; for example, we have been impressed that through the recent more open discussion of death, it can be looked at and talked about more freely, and thus the dreaded secret loses some of its threatening power. Moreover, because the feelings which are connected with these events can be acknowledged and integrated in the self, they may lead to a richer and fuller life. We wonder if the same would hold if incestuous fantasies could be more openly discussed.

There have been many studies about primitive *destructive* feelings, such as assault and murder, which present a great threat to the wellbeing of our society. Could it be that we have neglected to study difficulties which arise through essentially *loving* feelings but which nevertheless have primitive elements? Because of the horror of incest people shrink from accepting the benevolent aspects of a demonstrative affection between members of families in which incestuous longings are not allowed to take over and never threaten to subordinate the welfare of the child. In infancy and early childhood, close physical bonds of love with parents are vitally important, but we need to recognize that the child's healthy development involves growing free of these bonds. If the difficulty in attaining this freedom, both for the children and for the parents, can be acknowledged, then their secret longings can be more clearly understood, and the acting out of incestuous fantasies stemming from the infant's earliest feelings is much less likely to occur. Loving relationships between family members can then be enjoyed, despite their erotic components, without inappropriate anxiety and guilt.

5. The sensitivity of young adolescents to parental fantasies, and the parents' responses

We have tried to show the manifold developments which make the first five years of a child's life of such crucial importance for him and his family. The next stage in the life cycle for children between six and ten is relatively quiet in terms of emotional development, and appropriately called the latency period. If care and prevailing love are reasonably good, the child of six is comfortable enough in his relationships with the family to be quiet inside himself. He can turn some of his energies to the outside world which at this stage is represented chiefly by school with its friendships and by the sharing of interests with his peers. This is probably the reason why most contemporary studies of this age group tend to concentrate on primary education, a field in which much progressive and imaginative work is being done, but outside the scope of this book.

So in our exploration of the family life cycle, we shall move on to children in the age group between eleven and fourteen, the phase between childhood and adolescence when the boy or girl 'belongs at one and the same time to both stages without any longer being in the one, nor yet being in the other. What appears as an in-between stage is in fact a developmental phase that is set off both from what was before and what comes after.'[45]

As we have emphasized in Chapter 1, children of that age are often very puzzling to themselves and others. They grow fast and experience the first biological changes appropriate to their sex. The girl starts to menstruate and her breasts develop and the boy has his first emissions and wet dreams. These exciting and often worrying signs of biological development are not easy to assimilate and are usually accompanied by moodiness and the need to with-draw occasionally into the safety of infancy with quite startling expressions of regression.

Kate who had coped well with her first year at grammar school, had developed remarkable social graces, especially away from home, wanting to wear adult clothes for the 'dinner parties' which had replaced the children's tea parties; suddenly she had a compulsive need for a bedtime bottle. As she was too ashamed to buy one for herself she asked her mother to get her one 'for my dolls'. The mother accepted this request without questioning, and provided a bottle filled with milk every night. A few weeks later she was told in confidence of Kate's discovery that several of her classmates liked to go to bed with a bottle

Patrick, a tall, bright boy whose intellectual maturity had been much admired at school, burst into tears at tea time because a piece of cake he wanted was given to his little sister. When scolded for his childish behaviour he sobbed, 'But I am only eleven.'

Children of this age may be as ashamed and worried about their baby needs as about the new manifestations of their maturing sexuality. They begin to find that there are things in themselves and their lives about which they cannot talk and which they suspect to be also secret aspects of the other members of their families. Thus the early adolescent finds himself entering upon a new world of secrets and myths. A boy may go to any lengths to hide the sheets or pants which prove his emissions, not only because they recall shameful bed-wetting episodes but also because they may be associated with worrying dreams involving women who may perhaps symbolize his mother or sister. Both aspects are accompanied by mixed feeling about his new masculine potency and by a renewed feeling of powerlessness. His inability to control these unfamiliar impulses makes him want to keep his wet dreams a secret.

The girl who has started to menstruate and to develop breasts may be both proud and ashamed, and her secretiveness may be expressed in a different way and for another reason. She may hide her breasts by wearing brassières which are too tight or by a stooping posture, and will not listen to warnings that this is not healthy. Menstruation rouses very mixed feelings; it is hardly ever talked about directly but referred to as 'dirty', or called 'having the curse'; yet it is also greeted with pride. Now the girl has joined the ranks of grown up women and can share their secrets about sex and babies. She feels that her father has to be excluded from the secret; yet while it is important to her to pretend that he is not allowed to know, it is still more important that he should know. Twelve-year-old *Maureen* would try to play this double game by whispering into her mother's ear some news concerning her period in front of her father. In the presence of boys, girls indulge in endless giggling and whispers with each other about their secrets.

The new importance of boyfriend or girlfriend is another source of interest in secrets. The adults' often amused curiosity may add to the excitement about a romance, but also increases fears about being teased. If one talks to boys and girls of that age about their increased secretiveness, their reaction may be: 'We aren't more secretive, but the adults are more nosey.'

Maybe they are right, for we have noticed that in families with children of this age, the sensitivity of the children to their parents' sexuality is equalled by the parents' special sensitivity and curiosity about their children. If there is sexual dissatisfaction in the parents' marriage, this mutual curiosity can become obtrusive and disturbing. Parents who are dissatisfied in their sexual life are either excessively restrictive in defence of their own feelings or provocatively permissive in order to gain vicarious satisfaction through their children's sexuality. Either attitude makes it difficult for the children to come to terms with their own sexual and erotic development.

In the chapter on marriage we have talked about the secret and unconscious contract between the partners and the contradictory and confusing demands which they often make on each other. How far does this affect the development of their children? How does the next generation cope with such confusion and secrecy?

Although there is a vast literature on child development and children's problems, most studies are concerned with the individual child or with the relationship between parent and child, rather than with the multilateral interaction between the parents and all the other members of the family. Different schools of psychology put different emphasis on the importance of these family interactions compared with hereditary factors or with the child's personality and drive towards an autonomous development. There is however now an increased awareness of the need to examine a child's disturbed behaviour or sickness in the context of the interrelationships within the wider as well as the immediate family embracing perhaps even several generations.

In our work we have found that often children of the most disturbed marriages in which there are constant rows and dramatic scenes, are themselves relatively healthy, function well at school and socially, and seem little affected in their development by their parents' often childish and irrational behaviour. Often it seems that the children are more mature than their parents, albeit with a false maturity which can break down if the parents' marriage gets better and their behaviour more rational. In this safer situation the children may have a chance to regress, becoming more child-like and behaving more appropriately for their age.

In *Shared Phantasies in Marital Problems*[46] we described two very disturbed couples, the Smiths and the Donovans. The children in both these families seemed to be functioning well in spite of the frequent crises in the marriages and the parents' apparent inability to cope with their destructive impulses towards each other.

They were relatively free to develop their own personalities, their own identities, however much they may have been suffering from the stress at home. When parents are aware of their difficulties and are seeking help for themselves, the children arc under less pressure and less subject to the need to act out their parents' projections.

Where the parents' individual or marital problems are denied or suppressed, it is often the children who scream for help through symptoms of illness or disturbance, claiming attention for those aspects of their parents' personalities which they have not been able to develop themselves. For example, weak, frightened parents often have especially rebellious children who may express the anger and destructiveness which their parents have repressed. Or parents who are too timid and inhibited ever to take a risk in life may have a daughter like *Polly*.

Polly was a delightful child of eleven, bright, lively, popular but outrageously adventurous. She would climb the highest trees and jump from the steepest banks; her behaviour was a source of constant danger to herself and her many friends. For two years she had attended regularly and happily at a child guidance clinic and was liked by everybody there, but there was no change in her over-daring behaviour. Her therapist began to feel that this child's acting out might be modified if her parents, *Mr and Mrs Grant*, were drawn into the therapeutic situation, and advised them to consult a marital clinic. The parents who presented themselves as an ideal, united couple were puzzled about why they should need to consult an agency for marriage problems but they were determined to do anything which might help their daughter.

They were an outstandingly attractive couple who saw Polly's risk-taking as the only flaw in an otherwise perfect family. Mr Grant looked young for his age and held a job which seemed far below his academic and personal potential. When his social worker commented on this, he explained that this was the first job he had taken on completing his studies. He married as soon as he had qualified; as a family man he could not 'afford to take risks' and therefore it had never occurred to him to change jobs. This phrase, —'one cannot afford to take risks'—recurred constantly in discussion. He had met his wife, who was slightly older than himself, while he was still a student, and as he would not consider marriage until his income allowed him to offer her a good home, they were engaged for twelve years. She conceived soon after marriage, had a difficult pregnancy and confinement with Polly, and the doctors advised against having another child. On the grounds that no contraceptives were fool-proof, they stopped sexual intercourse.

Mrs Grant, an attractive, imaginative woman, was rather delicate and spent much of her time in bed with ill-defined ailments. Her bedroom, furnished in her favourite soft red colours, became the focal point of the house. When Mr Grant came home from work, he and Polly usually had tea by the mother's bed and later Mr Grant would keep her company and read poetry to her. The room which expressed the couple's artistic tastes, had nothing of the functional atmosphere of a sickroom, but suggested a setting for sophisticated lovers.

When alone, Mrs Grant spent her time writing science-fiction stories, which seemed to fill her need for adventure—just as the design of the bedroom was aimed to replace sexuality for her. All risk-taking and excitement of adventure was projected by both partners on to Polly, and we have seen how she acted it out.

Mr and Mrs Grant had very similar backgrounds. Both sets of parents were respectable, middle class people who lived carefully 'within their means'. Mr Grant was the eldest of three boys, Mrs Grant the eldest of three girls. Both felt that they had a special role in the family as their parents' favourites, and always tried to fulfil their expectations. In both families deviations from accepted patterns were not encouraged, conflicts were avoided, and the children had little opportunity to test out their own potential and different needs and drives. In neither home was sex ever mentioned. Both had received sex education from trusted family doctors. Neither had had

sexual experience before marriage, nor during their long engage-
ment. They felt that their sexuality like all other dangerous feelings
had to be kept well under control.

Polly seemed the perfect fulfilment of their dreams. She was a
beautiful healthy baby, always smiling, always happy. She was not
only the delight of her parents but of both sets of grandparents, for
whom she was for some time the only grandchild. She was seldom
naughty but already as a toddler showed an inclination to test
out her physical strength. She did it very cleverly and charmingly
without accidents and to everybody's admiration. Her parents'
attempts to send her to ballet school were defeated since she preferred acrobatics, at which she shone. Even when she began to
take risks, the parents were not immediately alarmed. It was their
neighbours and friends and Polly's teachers who brought it home
to them, that her adventures might be dangerous, and that it was
their duty to stop them. When not only they but also the child
guidance clinic, whose help they sought, failed to do so, the parents
became frightened. They felt that here was a force quite out of
control which threatened their carefully maintained defences
against risks. At the same time they could not really be angry with
Polly who was never rebellious, always loving and pleasant, and
seemed to act out of sheer exuberance. She seemed to be conveying
to them: 'Maybe I exaggerate, but I just want to show you something that you might like to do yourselves.'

It was surprising to see how quickly the whole family scene
changed once Mr and Mrs Grant began to feel that their therapist, in
contrast to their parents, trusted them to acknowledge and test
out their repressed needs for adventure and excitement without
fears of punishment or catastrophies.

The husband began to look for a better job; the wife looked
stronger and healthier; there were hints that the sexual relationship
had been resumed; and when Polly came home from an outing
complaining that a friend had taken such 'silly risks', the parents
felt that she—and they—were cured.

Therapeutic contact in this case was short, and it remains
uncertain whether the Grants will be able to convey to Polly as
she moves nearer to adolescence that she is free to develop her own
sexuality without having to take risks as a means of expressing
for her parents their inhibited sexuality.

In spite of these doubts we can see that the situation had changed sufficiently for these parents no longer to see Polly as their only problem. They were now aware that they themselves had problems, and were attempting to work on them.

The story of *Gloria*, shows how a child may feel herself driven to draw attention to the confusing messages about sex which come from the parents.

Gloria was fourteen years old when we first heard about her. She had been an only child until the age of eleven when, just as she left primary school, a brother was born and a year later a sister. Until then Gloria had been an easy child who fitted in well with all that was expected of her, both at home and at school. But when in both places she had to adjust to so many new situations, she became withdrawn, had few friends and her school reports deteriorated. She never talked about whatever bothered her, and her parents were too busy to find out. Her mother found it difficult to cope with the two babies especially when they turned into boisterous toddlers, and her father who had to earn more money for the growing family, spent longer hours at work and was hardly ever at home.

At fourteen she started to go out in the evenings without telling her parents and to stay out quite late. These escapades usually ended with her knocking at the door of some 'authority', a doctor, teacher, clergyman, even the police, and pleading in obvious distress, 'Please take me home, my father is going to thrash me.' When she was taken home, her worried parents could give no clue to her behaviour. Her father had never laid hands on her but wondered if perhaps that was what she wanted. To their anxious questions about where she had been and what she had done, the bewildered girl could only give the puzzling answer— 'I don't know, I just walked around.'

She was referred to the local Childen's Department (now the Social Services Department), and the young social worker on her first home visit to Gloria's family was puzzled by contrasting impressions. The home looked messy and uncared for. The father who was well dressed, quiet and polite, kept in the background. The mother dominated the sessions with lamentations such as 'Why does this happen to us? I come from a highly respectable home, grew up in a lovely, whitewashed, rose-covered country cottage. Why must I have a daughter who goes out at night, runs after every boy she meets, and brings disgrace on us?' The mother's evidence for Gloria's misbehaviour consisted of having once followed her and watched her flirting with the cobbler's apprentice through the shop window. Gloria listened in bewilderment to her mother's accusations.

At the weekly home visits which followed this first contact, the father did not reappear. Gloria was at school and the toddlers behaved in a most unruly manner, but the mother welcomed the social worker with much friendliness. She provided cups of tea and talked dreamily about the lovely rose-covered country cottage which seemed to be in such glaring contrast to her present situation. The social worker understood how difficult it was for this woman to give up her fantasy of an ideal home and waited patiently. After several weeks it emerged that the country cottage belonged to a newly married sister who had taken her in at the age of eleven when both her parents had died in a flu epidemic. The young couple were kind but had little patience with the bereaved confused girl. They were preoccupied with building their own life and their heightened sexuality was stimulating to the girl's erotic curiosity. As she could get no answers to her questions about sex in the home, she sought illumination in the village where she tried some sexual experiments with local boys. When she was sixteen she met her future husband whose army unit was stationed in the village. He was well-mannered and looked smart in his uniform. Her sister made him welcome and since, as an illegitimate child brought up in an orphanage, he had no relatives, he was delighted to be accepted in this friendly home. When the girl was eighteen, they married and had Gloria nine months later.

All went well until the husband left the army and the family moved to London, where he bought a café with his army gratuity. As shift work was prevalent in this district, he felt it important to keep it open at late hours. His wife, however, was convinced that it was used mainly by prostitutes and their clients, and she would often turn up at night scantily dressed to make a scene. When the husband could no longer tolerate this, he sold the café at a loss, and resentfully took a job with the Post Office. He tried to have little to do with his wife now, but these two lonely people were very dependent on each other, and by the time Gloria was ten they were trying to make a fresh start in their marriage, with the result that two more babies arrived . . .

As Gloria reached the age at which her mother had begun her sexual adventures in the village, the babies were becoming greedy, unruly toddlers. Both these developments stirred up the parents' unresolved conflicts about sex and control, and their shared anxious sexual fantasies were projected on to Gloria, who was in a state of adolescent confusion. Staying out late was her way of inviting an outside authority into the house to make sense of what she found bewildering; it seemed a cry for help for herself and her parents.

Neither parent had resolved his or her frightening fantasies about sex. For the father they sprang from his illegitimate birth and loveless childhood, while the mother's sexual confusion was aggravated by moving into the sexual atmosphere of her newly married sister's home, at the very time when she was disturbed by the loss of her parents and her home. Gloria's parents had never talked about sex to anybody, not even to each other. However, when the mother started to talk to the social worker about herself 'at Gloria's age', and about her own sexuality and guilt, she probably also broached the subject with her husband, because after keeping out of the way during the preceding weeks he suddenly decided at this point to change his shift work in order to be at home for the sessions with the social worker.

The story of their marriage with its hopes and frustrations emerged in conversation, and as the wife tried to understand her part in it, in relation to her past history, the husband, too, hesitantly began to talk about his life in the orphanage, his dreams about his mother and his wish to know what she and his father had been like. People had often commented on his 'refined appearance' and he began to build up a fantasy that he was of high class origin. Many questions preoccupied him. Why had his parents abandoned him? Had they loved each other? Had his mother suffered much in having him without a husband? Did sex ever bring happiness?

When this young couple married there had probably been an unconscious hope in both of them that together they could make sex good and give each other support in their loneliness. But their fears were deeply buried and they needed the help of the social worker to look at them. They began to see how they had used Gloria as a screen for their projections. At this phase in her development, Gloria had been especially susceptible, yet although she had exacerbated their sexual fantasies by her way of setting out to get help, she had managed to withstand acting out their fears in reality.

The background of Gloria's parents was similar in many ways; both felt abandoned, not belonging to the people they lived with, and both comforted themselves with fantasies of perfect homes and idealized parents. Both also shared their fears about the badness of sex. But in spite of these similarities they had developed very different attitudes and appearances, a fact which coupled with their shared fantasies about sex must have been most confusing to their daughter. That she withstood their joint projection and did not act out their sexual fantasies, but instead sought help for them, may indicate that she felt fundamentally unthreatened in her autonomy. Needless to say, both Gloria and her parents were unconscious of these processes.

It is well known that children unknowingly behave in an attention-seeking way in order to get help for their parents and themselves. We know of a case in which an eleven-year-old girl, *Pauline*, from an apparently highly respectable family, locked herself one night in a coal hole and then called to her neighbours for help. Her anxious mother took her to a child guidance clinic where the whole family was seen. On this occasion the father presented himself as a paragon of virtue, a reliable, conscientious man, who had an excellent work record. He was deeply concerned for his wife and children and said he had married his wife in order to rescue her from a drunken father and delinquent brother. He appeared anxious to participate in his daughter's treatment and asked for an appointment for himself in the following week. At this session, his previous self-vindication collapsed into an anxious confession to the social worker: he had in fact been out of work for some time, he was heavily in debt and afraid of eviction, but in order 'to protect my family, I have told nobody about this.' Yet his daughter Pauline must have sensed some of it and sent out a cry for help for her father. She could not confide in her mother, who unquestioningly shared the father's fantasy of himself as strong and virtuous, and of herself as being in need of his care and protection. Her image of herself was as false and unrelated to the reality of their life as that of her husband. Yet the whole family had colluded to maintain the myth of their father as a strong protector. It seems remarkable that children of this age group can have the sensitivity to respond unconsciously to their parents' secrets and the courage to get help for them quite on their own, without the support of an adult.

In all examples in this chapter, we have described the children's responses to their parents as if the parents were one person, despite their distinct attitudes and characteristics. The central factor to which the children respond seems to be the parents' unrecognized shared fantasies, especially their fantasies about sexuality. For the pubertal and pre-adolescent child who has to find his own identity and come to terms with his own sexual fantasies, the parents' shared confusion or anxiety about sex presents a threat for which the child is trying to get help by developing attention-seeking symptoms.

How far a child is able to fit in with the parents' shared fantasies will vary with the personality of the child. But children, just like marriage partners, can never be only the victim of the other's projections. For the parents' or the partner's projection to be accepted, it must also meet some inner need of the victim'. Children between eleven and fourteen may be too vulnerable to withstand their parents' attempts to use them as a vehicle for their own needs; in addition, their loyalty to the idea of a united family may be an important factor encouraging them to comply; nevertheless in order to serve the parents in the way they do, some of their own more selfish wishes are also being met. Here we have collusive interaction between parents and children, a collusive circle which often needs to be broken at some point to put an end to painful repetitions.

In the preceding stories we do not know enough about the parents' early histories to trace the origins of their sexual anxieties but we know enough to sense that their parents too, (the children's grandparents), had sexual inhibitions that made them unable subsequently to help their children through the ambivalent feelings of the oedipal phase. All these fathers and mothers therefore entered marriage with unresolved oedipal conflicts. It is remarkable with what unconscious certainty they chose a marriage partner whose emotional development was impeded during the same phase as their own. The unconscious hope expressed by such a choice of partner is likely to be that together the couple may be able to overcome the impediment, resolve the conflict, or learn to live with it and to grow in spite of it. We may call the pattern which they jointly set up in their marriage an oedipal collusion, and it is very likely to become reactivated during those phases of their children's life which are especially dominated by the children's own oedipal fantasies.

The age of early adolescence with its physical changes and reawakened erotic needs, together with a search for a separate identity, all inevitably serve to make this a critical phase in which increased conflict for both children and parents has to be expected. It is likely to stir up in the parents unresolved conflicts belonging to this or earlier phases in their own lives, which in turn may have repercussions on the children. In these stories we can see how the children were trying to cope with their own and their parents' conflicts, especially with half understood, open or hidden secrets about sexuality and about the parents' earlier life. The children's disturbing symptoms may be seen as attempts to express their confusions, and by doing so, motivate their parents to bring repressed feelings to their consciousness.

In early adolescence children are especially inclined to attempt to work out confusing and contradicting messages which come from the parents. They are doing this unconsciously in self-defence as at that age there is the risk that the child will feel his development being diverted by the pressure to fit in with the needs contained in the family secrets and myths. It is also the age at which children can find in themselves for the first time the ability and maturational strength to gain freedom from having to enact these myths and secrets, and thus may break the vicious circle that would otherwise limit their growth as individuals.

In these situations where the child carries the burden of the parents' problems and develops symptoms which arouse anxiety, the appropriate decision for teachers or people from the helping professions may seem to be to place the children away from home. But such a step, although it may appear to rescue the child from the parents' bad influence, may in fact result in the child not only pining for the parents, but feeling laden with guilt for having left them alone with their problems. If the child is removed from home, the underlying disturbance in the family relationships is rarely understood and cannot be modified. Quite often another child in the family will then take over the role which was held by the senior sibling. Also the removal of the overtly disturbed child defeats the purpose of his symptom if it expressed an attempt to get help for the family.

The story which follows illustrates how important it is for the growing process of the family to work out conflicts and pains within the family.

We learned about the *Adams family* when their younger son, *Tom*, was eleven, and his desperately anxious parents brought him to a child guidance clinic as a last resort for help with his severe eczema. They had tried everything else; special ointments, rigid diets, homeopathic medicine, taking him in and out of hospital, all without more than a brief alleviation of the eczema.

Tom, who clearly needed help in his own right, was offered therapy three times a week with a child psychiatrist, and his parents were offered casework help with two psychotherapists, Mr B and Mrs C, who decided to see them once weekly in conjoint sessions where both marriage partners and both caseworkers met together.

Tom was a pathetic figure, huddled in clothes two sizes too large for him, and covered in weeping weals of eczema. His frantic parents hardly saw him as a human being but in the words of his mother, as 'a screaming voice in the night, a tearing tangle of scratching hands, a weeping, wailing, furious ball of eczema on legs.' He was very angry, sulky and withdrawn, but eventually became willing to talk to a male psychiatrist. *Alan*, two years older than Tom, did not currently seem to be causing anxiety; and the Adams saw the problems as existing entirely in Tom. They could see no cause for his illness, but it soon became clear that the mother's relationship with Tom, whom she described as just like her, was based on a total lack of recognition of him as a separate being; rather he was an extension of herself, his pain was hers. If he had homework to do, she was driven by anxiety to help him and almost do it for him. She worked part time as a receptionist in a doctor's surgery and had her own diagnosis for Tom's condition. Plainly Tom's condition had some physiological basis, since he was born with it, but there was little doubt that additional causes had made it such a source of anxiety and brought him to this pitch of self-destructiveness during the last few months. The fact that two years before Tom's referral, the elder son Alan had been treated for severe asthma suggested that he too might suffer self-punishing symptoms, expressing the difficulties in the family. For we consider asthma to be 'the literal suffocation of the anger which cannot be expressed'.

The parents presented themselves as a happy hard-working

couple whose chief aim was to give their sons a good start in life. They saw themselves as quite unselfish in this endeavour, would never dream of having a holiday without their sons and altogether arranged their lives in such a way as to give the boys the best of everything. Mrs Adams put their case most forcefully to the clinic therapists. Her husband endorsed it fully, yet in a rather hopeless depressed way.

The Adams had no difficulty in talking about their apparently conventional backgrounds. Both came from Jewish families with much in common, including approval of the couple's choice of each other. They got on well with both their families and had bought a house in easy walking-distance from both sets of parents. Mr Adams was owner/manager of a small business which he had inherited from his father. Mrs Adams was a capable housewife in addition to having a part-time job. The two boys went to a local school. Everything was as it ought to be, and Mrs Adams, especially, had a great need to stress this fact. She was excitable and garrulous, could not tolerate silences and often seemed on the verge of paroxysmal laughter or hysterical tears at random. She did all the talking and presented the family as if it was hers alone. When Mr Adams was asked a question she answered for him, and he did not demur. She described Alan as 'just like his father', prone to hide his feelings but with 'lots underneath'; and Tom was just like herself, emotional and excitable. In spite of stressing these distinctions, Mrs Adams also insisted that she and her husband were like Siamese twins.

Their marriage clearly had positive aspects and allowed them to function 'happily' in spite of the fact that they had repeated to a large extent the pattern of interaction between their own parents, whom they saw as unhappy in their marriages. The Adams achieved their happiness by avoiding disagreement and denying the existence of any anger against each other.

In both the parental families, the mothers were the powerful dominant partners who made all the decisions. Both fathers were seen as gentle but passive and weak. Any initiative they did take, seemed to bring disaster to the family. Mr Adams' father had had a secret passion for gambling of which nobody knew until the terrible moment when it emerged that he had gambled the family's fortune away. Mrs Adams' docile father had secretly joined a group of conscientious objectors. When he was called up during the war he was so uncompromising that he had to serve a prison sentence, leaving his wife and small children without income alone in the London blitz. The feeling that men were useless, but if they showed any strength, it was destructive to their families, had become a family myth which was reinforced by the couple's experience with their brothers. Mrs Adams had had a brother three years younger than herself, who died when he was two years old. He would have been the only son in the family, and her mother had never stopped telling her that she had kicked her brother when he was tiny and that this was the cause of his death.

Mr Adams also had a brother who was four years older than himself. He was described as quiet and shy like all the men in the family, until suddenly in adolescence he began to develop a different personality and emerged quite a leader. He gained physical strength, loved to compete in sports and became a mountaineer. He died in a car accident when he was twenty-two.

Similar experiences with fathers and brothers, reinforced by shared experience of powerful mothers, greatly influenced the image that they had of themselves. Mrs Adams became a dominant woman as her mother had been, while Mr Adams kept passively in the background as his father had done. But despite this repetitive pattern there was some wish in them to have a different kind of marriage from those of their parents. Between the couple there was an understanding that in spite of Mr Adams' passivity he gave hints of hidden strength. His wife frequently referred to this, but made it quite clear that she wanted him to use these hidden powers only as she instructed him, for otherwise they would turn out to be disastrous for the family.

It is not difficult to imagine the contradictory feelings with which these parents greeted the birth of their sons. They were proud parents, who wanted their sons to be strong and successful, yet they were terrified of what would happen if this wish were fulfilled. If the boys should become 'proper men' and use their 'secret weapon' the parents were unconsciously convinced that they would kill themselves or ruin their families. Because of their own muddle these parents related and talked to their sons in a most confusing way, often contradicting what they had said by the way they said it. They could not tolerate the thought that their boys were growing up and that they would lose control over them. Until now the boys had done nothing on their own except go to school, where, so their parents' attitude told them, success was important but very doubtful of achievement. The boys were never dressed appropriately for their age. Their clothes were either too babyish or too adult. They were not allowed to look manly and were kept away from sports and games. Alan's asthma and Tom's eczema gave the overt reason for their parents to over-protect them, and forecast disaster for them. This created a vicious circle in which the boys were filled with unconscious anger by their own inability to combat their mother's intrusion into their lives and their father's inability to become their ally in protecting them.

Mr and Mrs Adams continued their joint sessions with their therapists for twelve months. Mrs B was an experienced family caseworker, while Mr C, who had analytic qualifications had never worked with families. At first, Mrs B took the lead but when Mr and Mrs Adams, who were used to discussing problems with their mothers and ignoring their father, readily accepted this set up in their sessions, Mr C felt ignored and found himself becoming resentful and withdrawn, just like the couple's fathers.

In short, the therapeutic pair colluded with the relationship pattern of the married pair, and while this state of affairs lasted there could be little hope of change. Yet when the two therapists became aware of this collusion and altered their behaviour to resist it the couple's immediate response was striking. After the first week of Mr C's more active participation and Mrs B's support for him, Mr Adams opened the session for the first time. He said that he strongly disagreed with the present arrangement to bandage Tom's hands to stop him scratching and offered to have a talk with both the boys who shared a bedroom. Tom should be made responsible for whether or not he scratched himself at night, might be given gloves to wear, but be free to use his hands. Mrs Adams responded to this entirely new acknowledgement of the boys' responsibilities with a hysterical fit, 'I won't do it. If Tom scratches himself to pieces you will go to work and leave me with all the mess and crying.' Mr C interpreted Mr Adams intervention as an attempt at saying, 'Tom isn't a baby and he is not dangerous. Leave it to him. I too can take responsibility even though I don't know what the outcome will be.' Except for pointing out Mr Adams' attempt to take his share of responsibility for family affairs the therapists left him on his own, thus supporting his autonomy and offering him a model for his own behaviour as a father. For the first time the couple compromised on a major issue. Tom wore gloves only in bed, and scratched neither more nor less, but the family situation had begun to change, and so had the pattern of the joint sessions. Mrs Adams became quieter and more able to listen to her husband and to Mr C, who together with Mr Adams began to take more responsibility for the work to be done in the sessions. The roles of men and women had changed both at home and in the sessions, and this made the couple look differently at the relationships with their own parents. The image of their mothers became less overpowering in their minds, and that of their fathers more loving. Their new and different experience of relationships with the parental figures at the clinic helped them to see how their inability to be independent of their parents had compelled them to deprive their sons of autonomy. They now attempted to modify this compulsive repetition that had dictated the relationship pattern of three generations. Alan, now nearly fifteen, was able to bring a girlfriend home and develop interests of his own. Tom was no longer a walking eczema case but a boy with an increasing identity of his own. His eczema improved and so did his school reports. Mr Adams became more effective and enterprising, and his increased self-confidence was also expressed in a new, more trusting relationship with his sons in which his wife was able to participate. She accepted that men might be able to take some initiative after all, and had herself become much more gentle and receptive. Their emotional relationship had changed, and there were indications that their sexual relationship which had hitherto been very infantile, had become more mature.

We might ask what had made for the remarkable changes in this family. It seems to us that once the therapists became aware of how much they had colluded with this couple's expectations they stopped doing so, and presented Mr and Mrs Adams with the task of re-examining the preconceptions on which their behaviour had hitherto been based. They had gained with the therapists an experience of parental relationships in which change was encouraged and proved beneficial. Feeling supported in their own autonomy they could risk being different from their own parents, and allow their sons their own identity.

Recent work in psychotherapy implies increasingly that the therapeutic process is seen as one of 're-parenting'.

Once this 're-parenting' has freed people like Mr and Mrs Adams from the stifling tie with their parents, and led them to discover their own potentials and limitations, they may continue this journey of self-discovery in their changing relationships, especially with their children, and thus break the vicious circle. To achieve this during their children's early adolescence is of particular importance because the development of children of this age is especially vulnerable to distortion by their parents' (mostly unconscious) expectations. It is also the age at which children are groping to find their own identity and seeking the ability to free themselves from the pressure apparently present to some degree in all families—to enact the family secrets and myths.

6. Later adolescence and identity formation

There is, we have seen, a great deal of psychological recapitulation of earlier crucial experiences, as the school-child goes through the pre-adolescent phase. In this period of life there is a particular need for the child to re-experience the pressures of feelings belonging to the oedipal phase, in order to resolve them so that the emotional life of the developing adult can take a direction outwards from the family of origin. After this phase, which is forced on the child both by his own sexual maturation and by the forceful expectations of society, there is still a great deal of psychological development to take place. This stage is adolescence proper.

During this time the individual has to give up childhood closeness and reliance upon parents, if he is to become really adult. At the same time, in order to preserve a sense of continuity and to feel properly rooted in his life, he must retain a loyalty to his family of origin. Giving up so much of the family-linked basis of the whole past life of the child is bound to be accompanied by a sense of loss and uncertainty, which in some ways can be seen as a mourning process. The search for a way of life that preserves a loyalty to the past—especially the past intense closeness to and dependence upon the parents while also developing an individuality that suits his psychological needs—will cause the adolescent uncertainty and discomfort too. For these two reasons adolescence can be a phase of life involving the experience of pain, loss and bewilderment. Winnicott[47] has used the phrase 'the doldrums' for the adolescent time but many other authors have also described the griefs and discomforts of the period.

The sadness of adolescence, and the demands of loyalty to the parents and the child's own past is shown in the story of twelve-year-old *Clifford Allen* who was referred to a child psychiatrist because he had been getting into trouble at school, lying, failing to do homework and had been cheeky in a childish way. He had had long episodes of enuresis through much of his childhood and was still occasionally bed-wetting at the time of referral. He had an older sister, Marjorie, who was fifteen.

In a series of family assessment interviews, leading to a conjoint family therapy, the therapist and the family learned that Marjorie was extremely miserable and in particular worried about growing up. We learned of the background to the problem. *Mr Allen* was the oldest child of a family of eight. His father, a miner, was not remembered as having played much part in his childhood. He knew that he had been upset when his mother had had four more children in five years, starting when he had been an only child of six years. He had been even more shocked when she had had a further three children after he had gone away to college at the age of eighteen. That had pushed him to decide to leave home. He did not consciously know why he had been so shocked by his mother's spread-out pregnancies that he almost completely cut himself off from his home.

Mrs Allen had had a contrasting upbringing. She had been brought up as an only child. She had been born illegitimate, and was convinced that her first two and a half years of life were spent in squalid poverty, from which she was saved by being adopted by a farming couple. When she was asked about her feelings concerning her adoption she said that she could not believe that she had grieved over the loss of her first mother because, she said, her life with her adoptive parents had been so loving and carefree. Her adoptive mother had fallen ill when she was fourteen, so that from the time of her early adolescence she had had to take quite a lot of responsibility in running the house and looking after her adoptive parents, but she did not consider that the happiness of her life had been spoilt by this. Her view was that they had taken her in and given her a lovely upbringing and home, and she was grateful of the opportunity to repay her debt. When she had met Mr Allen he had immediately taken to her parents, and they had taken to him. When it was suggested to Mr Allen that it was as though he too would like to have been adopted by the farming couple, he agreed. Mrs Allen said that in fact her adoptive parents would have liked a son and really did talk of Mr Allen as being like the son they themselves had not had. It is not surprising that when the couple married, they had a plan to have Mrs Allen's adoptive parents to live with them. Marjorie was born, and the couple now found that they were in a position to buy a house which they could offer to

Mrs Allen's beloved parents, as a home for their old age. They bought the house and Mrs Allen became pregnant with Clifford. But within a few weeks of each other her mother and her father died, and Mr and Mrs Allen's hopes of having the children's grandparents to live with them were dashed. Mrs Allen became extremely depressed, a state which her husband could not stand. Clifford was born and it is clear that at that time their estrangement nearly led to a broken marriage: Clifford's earliest life was clouded by these circumstances. Mrs Allen recovered slowly and the couple picked up the pieces of their marriage. But the original basis of the marriage had changed, for neither of them had wanted to give up life with her parents. We can see that Mr and Mrs Allen had, in different ways, both been precipitated rather early into adulthood, he by choice, out of anger with his parents for having more babies, and she because the illness of her mother required her to become a housewife at fourteen.

We would suggest that Mr Allen had withdrawn from his mother in what can be termed 'oedipal disgust'. Her frequent pregnancies showed that her sexual relationship with her husband was indubitably active and ongoing. Any persisting longings that Mr Allen had had from the age of his most active oedipal wishes, would have been continually affronted by his mother's pregnancies and the attendant body changes and psychological preparation. The intense physicality of birth and baby care had reminded Mr Allen of his former physical closeness to his mother and of the deep pleasure that it had given him. The force of his upset at the times of his mother's pregnancies included a reaction from the wishes for physical closeness to her, and instead repulsion to her body and hence a sense of 'oedipal disgust'. Further pregnancies in his adolescence, reawakening the same feelings, decided him to withdraw completely from the family. The changes in culture induced by his college education, to which his parents attributed his loss of contact was not a prominent reason. However the precipitateness of his withdrawal had left unfulfilled certain of his longings for closeness to his parents. Freud called the very common daydreams in which a child longed to find himself in a quite different family with a much more favoured status, 'the family romance'.[48] We would guess that in his primary school days Mr Allen may well have had daydreams of being adopted by comfortably-off parents who wanted an only son. When he met his future wife, it was something about her adoptive upbringing and the qualities of her adoptive parents which attracted him, as well as her homeliness and liveliness. When she became so grief-stricken at the loss of these specially valued parents, he too mourned grievously, and in addition could not bear her withdrawal from him. Perhaps he experienced it as reminiscent of his mother's withdrawals in her pregnancies.

We would also guess that Mrs Allen was not quite so untouched as she believed by the change of mothers she had had when she was two-and-a-half years old, for we know that children of that age suffer great pain at separation from the first person to whom they have been attached, even when the new mother is devoted and has much better material conditions to offer the child. Furthermore we know that such a separation is experienced as a catastrophe and that people who have suffered a loss as children are more predisposed, as adults, to be thrown into deep depression by further losses.

These aspects of the family history were fully discussed with both parents and with Marjorie and Clifford. The two children showed us how strongly they were worried about growing up and we thought that their worries were linked with an unspoken awareness of their parents' anxieties, and a fear that once you start to grow up, you either have to do it very suddenly, like Mrs Allen, or completely cut yourself off from your parents, like Mr Allen. When these things were put to the children and their parents, they were quite able to recognize them. Marjorie told us that she had been extremely miserable at that time, a year before, when her mother had had to go into hospital for a sudden surgical emergency. She had been convinced that her mother was going to die, but had not been able to talk to her father about it because she knew that he had not liked her mother talking of sad things. We then realized that Clifford's trouble at school had begun when his mother had been in hospital. It also came out that a lot of Clifford's fooling about at home and at school was part of a pattern in which he tried to cheer people up. This he did especially for his mother, who suffered miseries every spring, a sort of anniversary depression following her parents' deaths.

Mr and Mrs Allens' experiences in adolescence were not consciously known by the children. In fact Clifford had thought that his father had grown away from the paternal grandparents because he was clever at school. (It seems indeed that one reason why

Clifford was not doing as well at school as his intelligence would allow was his fear that, if he did, he would have to lose contact as his father had.) We would think that there was some unconscious sense in the children of the hazards of growing up that had befallen their parents and, following Mrs Allen's illness they had both found themselves responding to the increasing pressures of their biological growth by trying to resist the changes these implied and by feeling very unhappy. Discussion of these problems helped Marjorie to become much more cheerful and she began to develop the active social life necessary for approaching the tasks of growing up. Clifford became able to manage himself at school and was no longer thought of as a childish nuisance.

Once the adolescent is able to overcome the most intense reservations about beginning to move towards adulthood he begins to find himself searching and experimenting with modes of life, varieties of attitudes, religious and political beliefs, jobs or professions, leisure activities, love objects and sexual relationships, as he tries to find those that suit him and express himself. Erikson[49] has called this process 'identity formation', (see Chapter 1). In particular Erikson[50] draws attention to the effort of the adolescent to find a way of life that expresses his needs to become an independent adult whilst at the same time utilizing what he terms 'the effective remnants of his childhood'.

Mr Allen's choice of love object, in the person of his wife, had been conditioned by disappointment he had felt with his own mother. The next example shows an initial choice of profession influenced by what were essentially oedipal conflicts.

James Martin had wanted to become a priest when he left home, and entered a seminary at the age of eighteen. After ten years he came to the conclusion that the decision had been a wrong one for him and he left the priesthood. Some years later he was able to recover in psychotherapy some of the reasons for the choice of career made in adolescence.

He was the elder of two brothers and had no sisters. His parents were both born in Ireland and his father in particular had had an extremely difficult early life, leaving home to earn a poor living at the age of fourteen. His parents had married in their thirties, when the father had established himself as a more skilled worker. James had memories of his father from the first few years of life but knew

that then there had been a gap in his contact with his father while
he was in Ireland with his mother and his father worked in wartime
England. He had looked forward to the reunion with his father,
but when that took place he found that his father was so injured,
in some way that this small child never fully understood, as to be
a virtual cripple for the next few years. He was profoundly disturbed
by this. He realized that his mother was extremely contemptuous
of his father and always critical of him for bringing too little money
home. James' younger brother had been born when he was four,
shortly after his mother and father were reunited in England, and
though his father was gradually recovering his full vigour, James
thought that his mother and father never regained the love and
happiness with each other that seemed to have been their relationship before the wartime injury. The family developed a split in
which he, James, found himself siding with his father, and his
brother always sided with his mother. This can be understood to
have been an abnegation on James' part of his possession of his
mother after the birth of his brother, but his attempt to find
security in identification with his father was made difficult by his
father's injury and then by the realization of the mother's contempt
for his father. Although he did not give up ambition for physical
prowess he came to rely more on his established cleverness for his
place in the school world. However his link to his father had to be
rather secret because it would expose him to his mother's contempt,
and in his teenage years he discovered a way to be close to his
father and yet also to replace him and to get a special closeness
to his mother: he announced his vocation for the priesthood. This
achieved many things. In the first instance his mother was extremely
devoted to and respectful of priests. She was an ardent churchgoer
and showed her respect for priests but also treated them in a slightly
coquettish way. She achieved great status in the parish by her
son's ambition. Further, by becoming a priest he could take
his place as a 'father' without having to become sexual. He had
early learned that there was some failure in his parents' loving
relationship and it seems likely that he had, as a child, fantasized
that his father's injury and his mother's anger at her husband were
in some way connected with a failure in his father's effective masculinity. But he also had reason to know from his mother's expressed
attitudes that she disapproved of male sexuality. The decision to
become a priest enabled him to evade, totally, the possibility of

having to expose his masculinity either to a woman's scorn or to her revulsion. Moreover he could outflank his usurping younger brother and be special to his mother again. His brother was unimpressed, but that was not enough to deter James from his vocation, any more than was his father's lukewarm attitude.

He became a priest and was well thought of by his parishioners and the hierarchy, but after a while he realized that in fact he had no real wish to live his life without physical heterosexuality. He left the priesthood and soon married.

We make the following interpretation of the story. We think that James Martin's adolescence shows how uncomfortable secrets led him to spend ten years of young adulthood in what turned out to be a detour from his later self. The secret of the nature and origins of his father's injuries and of his parent's relationship had a profound effect upon his adolescent attitudes towards his own developing sexuality. In his mysteriously impaired father he could not find a reliable pattern of adult sexuality, while his mother's scepticism of his father's value made him further distrust the possibility of feeling comfortable in a fully masculine role. His conscious knowledge of his mother's overt attitudes to the church and the priests also clearly played into his unconscious, oedipal needs for closeness with his mother. Even so, it is clear that he did not feel his seminary and priesthood days to be all loss, and he eventually became a happy and comfortable husband and father.

Parental attitudes to adolescent offspring profoundly affect the feelings and optimism of the youngster entering into adulthood. Bowlby[51] has expressed a view of the optimal attitude and capability of parents towards the adolescent movement of their children: '. . . the family experience of those who grow up to become relatively stable and self-reliant is characterized not only by unfailing paternal support when called upon, but also by a steady yet timely encouragement towards increasing autonomy, and by the frank communication by parents of working models—of themselves, of the child and others—that are not only tolerably valid but are open to be questioned and revised.'

Nathan Ackerman,[52] whose innovative work with whole families had made him one of the best known practitioners of family therapy, has expressed a more pessimistic view of the nature of the effect of parental attitudes on youths going through the adolescent time, 'Inevitably disillusioned in the standards of his parents and society, the adolescent searches for new and more satisfying standards. From among the diverse extrafamilial groups, he makes a choice. He does so in accordance with the vicissitudes of his changing concept of self and the outer world. To replace the shattered ideal of his parents, he seeks a new one.'

We wish to stress both the discomfort of this search and also our belief that the young person's self as he explores and develops it will continue to include those aspects of the self that have been shaped by the longstanding relationship with the parents, which in our view are not so much shattered as shaky and which need reworking.

Ralph at the age of fifteen seemed to be a boy who was going through a deep depression accompanied by that total loss of sense of direction that is often characteristic of adolescents, and can cause utter despair in their families.

To the intense pride of his parents up to now he had done very well at school. He was near the top of the class in every subject, and played football and cricket for the school. He had begun to attract girls and he had many friends. Quite suddenly he stopped going to school. He said he was bored and there was no point in going. His parents were uncomprehending and despairing. He lay around all day, reading paper backs and listening to pop music.

During family therapy it became clear that the roots of Ralph's extreme ennui and disillusion were certainly partly linked to the wide areas of emptiness and timorousness in his parents' lives. For example it came out that they had very few friends, did very unexciting things in their holidays and recreation time and their jobs were both repetitive and dull. They gradually came to realize that in fact there were more interesting and lively pursuits they could follow and this helped Ralph himself. But months of work were needed before he could enjoy finding a more expansive life for himself.

The idealism and optimism of adolescents provides an excitement and a freshness to each generation but there tends to arise an opposition, on the part of parents in particular and society in general, to the vigorous hopes and aspirations of adolescents. Edith Buxbaum[53] points out:

Society's distaste for adolescents is reflected in its ambivalence towards them. On the one hand, they treat them like children, on the other, they expect them to behave like adults. The adolescent, expressing drives that adults have had to repress, reminds them of themselves and makes them acutely uncomfortable. Hence the wish that the adolescent would grow up and get over it.

The repressed drives and wishes of the adult, which the adolescent may be expressing, constitute what we are calling the secret life of the adult. They can, as we have seen in so many examples, be expressed in families by the spouse or children. Buxbaum draws attention to the ambivalence of society, (and of course of parents), towards youngsters. As we have shown with our first example in this chapter teenagers whose behaviour indicates their own ambivalence to growing up can at the same time be expressing any secret ambivalence the parents may have had to their own growing up during adolescence. As the children make their moves towards adulthood they will have to meet their parents' reawakened ambivalence towards such attempts, redoubling the arduousness of the children's task.

An extreme example of a young person totally failing, over many years, to make any move into adulthood, came to light in the family of a lady of fifty, who was put on probation for shoplifting.

While making his enquiry for the court report on *Mrs Ilford*'s shoplifting, the probation officer discovered that she had a twenty-one-year-old daughter, whose problems were much greater than her own. *Lucy* was virtually housebound by a number of obsessional rituals concerning washing her clothes and hands. These apparently prevented her from going out of the house to work, to enjoy herself or to meet friends. Mrs Ilford was the only person whose food and washing Lucy would accept. On top of this Lucy was extremely intolerant of her mother's departure from the house for any reason, and had been known to run down the road after her mother's bicycle, screaming 'Mummy please don't go.' The probation officer also had thought that the other child of the household, *Roger*, aged twenty-five, although not so extreme in his dependence as his sister, none the less was rather too much of a 'stick-in-the-mud' for a young man of his age, was not constantly employed and had little life outside the family. Roger had a reasonably equable relationship with his parents and sister, but Lucy had an extreme aversion to her father. At all costs she would avoid any physical contact with him and tried as hard as possible not to talk to him. On an occasion shortly after her mother's shoplifting had brought the family affairs to the probation officer's attention, when the father had tried to restrain Lucy from clinging to Mrs Ilford who wanted to go out, Lucy attacked her father with a bread knife.

The family dated Lucy's disturbance to a time when she was nine years old and had got lost on the beach and separated from her father for twenty minutes. There was some suggestion that there might have been some 'sexual goings-on' on the beach but there was no hint that Lucy had been assaulted, just a suggestion that she might have 'seen something'.

The probation officer was certain that Mrs Ilford's offence must derive from the manifest problems in the family, but felt uncertain of his competence to cope with Lucy's problem as it had so many features which he considered 'psychiatric'. He saw Mrs Ilford in accordance with the court order and she committed no further offences. He heard a great deal more from her about the rows and disturbance in the family and eventually decided to try to gain more understanding of the situation by seeing the family together. In the family interviews he was impressed by the extent to which the family was dominated by Lucy. He felt that Roger was really very much left out of the family activities but that *Mr Ilford* too was cut off from his wife by Lucy's demands and resorted to constant reading and listening to his records. However Mr Ilford openly expressed the view that his wife's relationship with his daughter was incestuous and that his son and daughter also had an incestuous relationship. He at no time considered the possibility of there being a sexualized relationship between himself and his daughter.

Mrs Ilford described her mother as a secretive and roundabout person, which was rather the impression that she herself gave. She said that her father was taciturn and moody, and that he was controlled and manipulated by his wife. It struck the probation officer that the Ilfords' marriage resembled that of Mrs Ilford's parents as she described it. However Mr and Mrs Ilford said there were no marital problems other than those brought about by rows over Lucy.

The probation officer felt that the family was being dominated by the difficulties with Lucy and thought that there was probably more of a marriage problem than had been admitted to, but was uncertain of how to proceed. He believed that Mrs Ilford's difficulty had been a signal of the family distress and sought psychiatric consultation. It was put to him that the repulsion between Lucy and her father looked as though it was 'counter-oedipal'. Heightened longings of a daughter for her father, dating from the oedipal stage of childhood, are of course to be expected in adolescence, yet Lucy, by protesting that she hated her father and could not bear to talk to him, let alone touch him, seemed to be trying to deny any possibility of such feelings towards him (cf. Sheila in Chapter 4). Her father had volunteered the suggestion that a variety of incestuous wishes existed in the family but made no mention of the most obvious and likely one, that between himself and his daughter. It was pointed out that Mrs Ilford, being post-menopausal, might well have had strong feelings of rivalry for a sexually active daughter, but instead her daughter made it clear that it was mother that she wanted, not men.

After a while Mr and Mrs Ilford began, for the first time, to talk about their long-standing difficulties, in particular the probation officer heard about the problems they had had in talking openly and directly to each other about Mrs Ilford's jealousy of her husband's flirting with her older sister. The probation officer was now in a position to talk to the family about the real incestuous feelings that dominated the situation—briefly those between Lucy and her father. He believed that these had excited in Mrs Ilford an unavoidable reminiscence of the painful frustration in childhood and adolescence of her oedipal longings for her own father, which could find no satisfaction in a family where she always came second to her elder sister. Lucy's abnormal behaviour was an increasingly exaggerated and desperate attempt to deny the existence of feelings that she was unconsciously aware would cause her mother such disturbance.

We are trying to show that the persistence of extreme oedipal problems can cause great interruption of the movement of an adolescent into adult ways of life, in which they can find a relative degree of independence from the family of origin together with a capacity to form attachments and independence within a new circle of relationships of a sort that will lead towards loving relationships and mature parenthood in their turn.

Jacobson[54] has summarised the development of the adolescent phase thus

> The oedipal child has to repress his sexual and hostile impulses in favour of affectionate attachments to his parents. In adolescence the sexual maturation process leads to a temporary revival of pre-oedipal and oedipal instinctual strivings thus reviving the infantile struggle. But now the incestuous sexual and hostile wishes must be finally relinquished. Moreover, the adolescent's affectionate ties to his parents must also be sufficiently loosened to guarantee his future freedom of object choice and to permit him a sound reorientation toward his own generation and a normal adjustment to adult social reality. This is the cause of his grief reactions.

The pre-oedipal and oedipal times have their impact on later development, and in particular on the adolescent time. Just as the oedipal phase is affected by the pre-oedipal time, so is the adolescent influenced by the infantile and intervening period of the child's life. But in the adolescent time the child has also had to cope with versions of the infantile conflicts that have been revived in the pre-adolescent sexual maturations. Processes go on in adolescence which enable the young person to revive old problems and rework them, finding fresh solutions which satisfy needs without damaging relationships. Insufficient working out of these processes makes it difficult for the person to undertake any move into adulthood. Later object choice, job choice, cultural, political, religious and leisure identities will show the imprint of the attempts to achieve separation from the earlier strivings whilst retaining elements of those strivings.

The balance between the old and the new in the achievement of adolescence is expressed in terms of loyalty by Ivan Boszormenyi-Nagy:[55] 'Emancipation from the overdependence of childhood hinges on the success of the adolescent's attempts at rebalancing loyalty obligations. . . . Throughout maturation the adolescent must learn to discount rigidly binding obligations for repayment of the parents' availability and services. Without a "liberation" from such obligation the adolescent is not able to free himself and use his potential e.g., in the process of evaluating and committing himself to peers and prospective mates.'

The new balance, he goes on to say, takes a 'prolonged process of *negotiation of compromises*' between the adolescent and his parents, and sudden acts of self-destruction or physical separation from the family may be attempted by the youngsters in order to by-pass this taxing process.

A rather unusual, almost bizarre example of a young man who attempted to escape from a very particular and painful family situation, by entering into a marriage of very marked characteristics, had the following outline. The young man, *Henry*, was aged nineteen when he married a girl who was well known to be the local 'loose woman'. She lived next door and so her sex life could have been no secret to him. However he was escaping from a family with an extremely rigid, painful and destructive pattern imposed by the marriage of his agoraphobic mother to his violent and pathologically jealous father. If his mother's phobic symptoms improved, she could go out more, but then her husband's jealousy would heighten and marital attacks would escalate. Henry's sister Alice, aged fifteen, was also confined to the house by anxieties that closely reflected her mother's, and was totally unable to go to school or go out with her friends. She acted as a companion for her mother and as her father's spy, chaperoning her mother. Henry needed an outside relationship to escape this dreadful situation. To marry a girl whom he had every reason to suspect of sexual infidelity paradoxically freed him from the family problems of violent and self-torturing jealousy : there would at least be no tormenting doubt about the feared betrayal. Although the outcome of the relationship was not known to us, the marriage may have been Henry's only way of getting away from the intense pain of his family.

We have not described here the very regular struggles between teenagers and their parents about dress, company, bedtime habits, drinking, hair length, and so on that are characteristic of family life with teenagers. We know that these issues are often the subject matter of disputes between youngsters and their parents. Along with personal and political views, opinions about neighbours and relatives, social values and pop music, they are fought over and argued about throughout early and later adolescence until the younger person knows that his parents accept his right to have his own views. Eventually, for the relationship to reach a stable state, the adults have to accept the older adolescent's views, opinions and life style almost as if he were an unrelated adult in the family. If this acceptance cannot be achieved, so that the fighting has to continue, the adolescent must either leave the family or stay in it at the cost of failing to complete the process of going through adolescence and of becoming an adult.

Much of the popular view of adolescence is that it is a stage of rebellion in which young people strive to achieve independence in the face of repressive opposition. No adult ever loses the need for close and caring attachments and there can be no question of an adolescent losing such needs overnight. His memory of his recent dependence leads him to need to *assert* independence as though against intense opposition. Parents often respond by opposition sometimes against their conscious will, for they remember their own adolescence being marked by similar struggles with their own parents. The opposition frequently has the appearance of being ritualized. To achieve separation the adolescent often has to repress a very conscious knowledge of childhood love and longings for closeness in order to overcome the pull of oedipal longings and to achieve an escape velocity high enough to get out of the family orbit. The overt picture of rebellious striving for independence can be seen to contain elements of a cover-up of the secret wishes to prolong a childhood closeness. As Talcott Parsons[56] has pointed out from the standpoint of the sociologist, the incest taboo is needed to ensure exogamy, so that there can be an intermixture of culture and genes between families.

At one level it is the incestuous solution to relationship needs that the adolescent must struggle against. At another it is the need to strive for an independent personality with uniqueness, individuality and separateness that pushes the youngster out of the family and into his own life and relationships. Parents have to be there for support, encouragement and love, but also to be fought against. A number of authors have pointed out that a 'permissive' parent, who wants to join in with the adolescent, is not being helpful. As Deutsch[57] puts it:

In previous generations the parents were 'in the other camp'. They sought to *counteract* the efforts of their adolescent children to free themselves from their dependency by actively loosening their ties to home. In the contemporary struggle between generations, however, the problems are more complicated. Many parents—especially mothers—have a strong desire to be 'modern' too: they show 'tolerance', abdicate their parental authority, and even go so far as to collaborate in the rebellious activities of their children.

One problem is that children become adults in a world which is in many ways different from the one within which their parents went through adolescence. Adolescent expectations and experiences may therefore seem especially strange to many parents. Spiegel[58] has shown how emigration creates what he calls 'role-conflict confusion', for the children of emigrant parents become adolescent in the life and ways of the new country while their parents recall an adolescence separated not only by generation but by space and a change of cultural context also.

These social changes are fundamental and at times devastating but we emphasize here elements of adolescent-parent relationship which we think stem from some basic ways of human relatedness. They centre upon the solution of the ties, rivalries, longings and fears of the oedipal situation and its impingement through adolescence and beyond. The secrets and shared fantasies which we are attempting to describe seem to us to exist essentially on that deep level, although they find expression in forms influenced by social customs and conditions.

7.   Marriage and the midlife crisis

For each generation marriage, the origin of a new family, is also a cradle for secrets stemming from universal fantasies about sex, birth and death, love and hate, and the fears and longings they embody. There may be times when the secret fears and wishes are apparently dormant but they nevertheless strongly affect everybody's life, and most especially during those phases in the life cycle which are marked by a transition from one pattern of living to another. Such transitional phases involve change and hence may contain the potential for crises.

The turbulent phase of adolescence with its special anxieties both for the young people and their families sets the stage for one of the major phases of transition. The young people are aiming at independence, leaving home, searching for sexual partners, and beginning to think about marriage and a family of their own. The eternal cycle begins all over again.[59]

As each child reaches adolescence his parents are reminded that eventually they will again be on their own. A renewed twosome can reveal the strength of their marriage and bring increased closeness, but it can also highlight those of the couple's needs which were less apparent while the children were at home. The marriage of the first and the departure of the last child from the family home may create a specific crisis which may precipitate the parents' task of making a midlife appraisal of their achievements and failures, a task they may well fail to recognize or seek to avoid.

What we call 'midlife' may last for several decades, and may make itself felt for each couple at a different point; and as the changes in the family situation may go on over some time, it is difficult to determine the right moment for a midlife appraisal. Attitudes to ageing are undergoing a fundamental change. Middle-aged people can now feel and appear young and this plays into their wish to deny the inevitable approach of old age. At the time when the children are leaving home and perhaps starting families of their own, the parents, now incipient grandparents, may be in their fifties, still looking and feeling in their prime. The increasing expectation of a long life span which can mean that several decades of married life still lie before them, adds new aspects to post-parental marriages.

J. Marmor writes, 'The manner in which these normal stresses in middle life are dealt with in men and women depends upon factors which are highly personal and idiosyncratic. Generally speaking, the weaker the ego-adaptive capacity, the more limited the base of interpersonal relationships, the narrower the foundation of the sense of usefulness and the interest in the outside world,—the more critical will be the impact of the middle years' stresses.'

These stresses are likely to be more strongly felt in small isolated families than in those settings in which the extended family still plays an important part.

In the professional and middle classes the successful husband will at that time have to bear the burden of his success. He will be perpetually busy with continual demands being made on his energy and time, which leaves little of either for his wife and family. Yet while he may be at the peak of his success, he cannot ignore the threat of younger, more virile men who will be his successors. His anxiety about lessening potency may lead him to seek reassurance and stimulation from young women.

The wife's menopause may coincide with a daughter's pregnancy; or she may put on weight and feel sexually unattractive just when her daughters are radiating sexuality. The mother may be confused by her mixed feelings, rejoicing in her daughters' successful femininity but depressed and jealous because of her own decline. All these stresses can have far-reaching effects on the family relationships.

While in the professional and middle classes the husband may be overwhelmed by the demands of his work, in most manual jobs the man's work capacity, and with it the income, begins to decrease just at the time when the son's work and earning capacities are rising. The father may have worked hard to give his son better chances in life than he had himself and yet may envy the very success which he has helped him to achieve and with which he can no longer compete. The roles have changed and few unfulfilled aspirations are now likely to be realized. Depressive feelings may be augmented by physical changes, diminishing sexuality and the prospect of approaching retirement. Fears of loss and death are reinforced by increasingly frequent serious illness and death in the extended family and among contemporaries. All this takes place against the background of a society in which youthfulness is admired and old age brings little of the respect which has graced it in other times and cultures.

On the other hand, if jobs and marriage are on a sound foundation, then middle age may be a time in which both marriage and jobs can come to full maturity. The growing number of apparently happy and lively golden wedding pairs indicates that if the hurdles of the midlife crises can be overcome by acceptance rather than by denial, then getting old can bring new satisfaction and enrichment and a fresh bond between the couple. Midlife, like any other life crisis, is a crucial point of increased vulnerability and heightened potential.

There are, however, couples who have never felt secure with each other, and those who feel that their marriage has not been sanctioned by their parents may be particularly prone to doubting the value of their union. In periods of change and stress, such couples need the support of a wider family, of friends or their community. If this is missing they may turn to a helping agency.

One such couple, *Mr and Mrs Turner*, who had felt 'cursed' by the wife's mother, considered separating when their only daughter, loved and admired by them both, was about to get married. They felt that without this daughter their marriage was meaningless, and each felt that each had failed the other. But with the help of their caseworkers they were able to acknowledge that there might be some good in their relationship as they had been able to produce such a good daughter. When thinking about their marriage without her, however, they could only envisage that she would still serve as a bond between them and that in some measure they could still have a share in her life.

On the day before the wedding Mr Turner came to rehearse with his caseworker the speech which he was to give as the bride's father. As he left he asked her to send a greetings telegram on the wedding day and when she wondered to whom he hesitatingly replied, 'To the new couple.' This she did, knowing that it was really meant for himself and his own wife. The following day he telephoned to report that all had gone well, and that he would now take his wife for a holiday, adding half jokingly: 'A sort of honeymoon.'

When they returned home there was considerable friction in spite of their attempt to make a new start. The husband compared his daughter's loving care for her husband with his wife's indifference towards him. The wife compared her son-in-law's consideration for his wife with her husband's lack of concern for her. In spite of their bickering, however, there was no doubt that the Turners were trying to find a new model for their marriage. They regained new value for themselves and each other by having found a new model in their daughter's marriage, and in their therapists, parental figures who had given them their blessing.

What happened in this marriage may be understood in different ways: the crisis before the daughter's wedding can be seen as Mr Turner's difficulty in letting his daughter go; his identification with the bridegroom as a renewal of his oedipal rivalry; his wife's anger with her husband as an expression of her jealousy of his love for their daughter. Or we may feel that to help his daughter to a good marriage and give her the blessing that was missing in his own, made Mr Turner feel worthy and good enough to renew the bond with his wife. Probably there is something in both these interpretations; Mr Turner gained some satisfaction through his daughter's happiness as well as through his ability to renounce her, and this renunciation made it possible for his wife to want to make a new start.

The wedding ritual in our culture underlines the fact that the daughter never belongs to herself; she belongs either to the father who gives her away or to the husband to whom he gives her. It seems astonishing that there is no part in the ceremony for the bridegroom's father or for either mother. For the father this ritual can involve considerable strain which is sometimes physically demonstrated in illness, heart attacks or even death, following soon after a daughter's wedding, in which the father has not only to let his daughter leave home but also to renounce his own unconscious incestuous fantasies and longings.

The story of *Mr and Mrs Shepherd* also shows what the daughter's departure from the family can mean to the parents. The couple were urgently referred for therapy by a university department in which Mrs Shepherd was doing a post-graduate course. She had reacted violently to the discovery that her husband was having a love affair with his young secretary. The couple were both aged fifty, had been married for twenty-seven years and had two children, a son who was studying abroad, and a daughter who had recently married. The wife had been working in a legal centre and now that the children were no longer at home she wanted to gain additional qualifications. The husband was a civil servant in a useful but uninteresting job, which he felt to be inferior to his wife's.

In the first therapeutic session Mrs Shepherd herself linked her husband's affair with his secretary with his love for his daughter, which, she said had always been unhealthy. In a very agitated way she went on to say that this unhealthy relationship was not surprising because of his home background. He was an only son with one younger sister and his dominant mother still treated him as if he were her little boy. His father was a weak person who would run after any woman including herself if his wife did not keep a watchful eye on him. Now he was in his eighties and senile, and his wife literally locked him into the attic to stop him from running after girls. Mr Shepherd listened to all this demurely, almost without comment. The therapist had difficulty including him, as well as breaking into Mrs Shepherd's torrent of abuse. It did however emerge that Mrs Shepherd despised her weak mother and wanted to be like her exciting and dominant father, whose role in the family she took over whenever he was absent. Her gentle and passive husband had obviously replaced his dominant mother by a dominant wife. In spite of the present crisis situation it became clear that the couple were very fond of each other, and while the children were at home their marriage had worked well, with both partners continuing the roles which they had developed in their parental families. But having to give away his attractive daughter was a severe loss for Mr Shepherd and he tried to find solace with his young secretary who admired him and offered him the affection which he just then so badly needed. His wife's hysterical and threatening response to his affair made him want to run away from her. He was unable to understand that her extreme anxiety expressed not only her fear of losing her husband but also of losing the role which had been familiar to her from childhood.

After a particularly dramatic scene between the couple, both agreed that they could not go on living together and Mr Shepherd gained his wife's consent to visit his girlfriend who lived outside London, and offer to make his life with her. This meeting turned out very differently. The girlfriend was disturbed because an uncle who had been a father substitute to her was now dying of cancer. Mr Shepherd realized that whereas she had wanted him as a father, he had wanted to marry a daughter substitute. He also became aware that his wife had replaced his mother in his life and therefore had not helped him to give up his dependence which he resented. He also realized that he had failed his wife, by not giving her sufficient support in her attempts to give up her identification with her controlling father. Both felt it was not too late for them to help each other, if they could now share this insight and resolve to begin a new life together.

When seen again five years later the couple had succeeded in this to an outstanding degree; both looked quite different, he stronger, she more gentle. Their life was full of plans and hopes and they insisted that this was so because they had learnt so much from their midlife crisis.

Of course there are couples whose only investment in their marriage has been their children and who feel they have nothing else in common. Without their children, the marriage has become flat, the couple frustrate each other and their sagging vitality is likely to affect all other areas of their lives. Conflicts which were hidden while the children were at home may now become unmanageable or lead to illness. In situations like this, life with a new partner may restore vitality, and once the children are no longer dependent on their parent's relationship they too may benefit from having happily separated parents rather than frustrated ones living together. A view which has recently been widely discussed stresses that these unsatisfied post-parental couples whose marriages have lost vitality, might gain new happiness and become useful members of their communities if at that stage 'the spouses re-assorted themselves with new partners.' But such suggestions may ignore the developmental possibilities of post-parental marriages. If, for example, the two couples already described had parted, they might have been confirmed in their own worthlessness. In fact we have seen that their attempt to learn something from their failures and make a new start on the basis of that insight was felt as an achievement which gave them new confidence to overcome difficulties.

Mr and Mrs Forester are another example; the husband, somewhat older than his wife, was a quiet man who could not assert himself and who had colluded with his wife in giving up an active part in the family when their son was born. The son who was handsome, intelligent and musical (a gift which incidentally he had inherited from his father) became the centre of his mother's life. She idolized him and did her utmost to create a hostile relationship between father and son. We can guess that this mother had an unconscious fantasy that it was her son and not her husband who was the man in the house and to whom she wanted to be married. When the boy was seventeen and had turned into a tall and attractive young man the situation aroused anxiety in both mother and son, and at the same time the hostility between father and son became more openly expressed. It was ostensibly to protect the boy from his threatening father that the mother asked with great urgency for help.

Very early in the therapeutic contact it became clear that this woman was frantic because she felt herself to be on the brink of disaster. It was as if she had suddenly become aware of her involvement in an oedipal tragedy in which she was expecting her son to become her lover and kill his father.

When she could face some of this with her therapist, she suddenly and surprisingly asked for help with her marriage. Her husband's inclusion in the therapeutic process was a first acknowledgement that he had a part in the family, and led quickly to quite astonishing changes in the couple's relationship. It also led to the son's decision to emigrate to Canada where his mother's sister lived. It seems as if he had become painfully aware of the way he had colluded with his mother by keeping his father out and claiming his mother for himself.

His mother grieved deeply over his loss; her husband found a new role for himself by comforting her, and this was the beginning of a new bond. When mother visited her son, she found him happily settled; after her return home, she began to discover new aspects of her husband's personality which she had refused to acknowledge before. She was then actually able to say that she was now grateful that her son had left in time so that his loss could become a gain for their marriage.

The midlife crisis of the Foresters had provided a turning-point in which all three of them were able to find a satisfying outcome instead of disaster.

Even without such dramatic development many post-parental marriages become more rewarding and gain fresh impetus in a renewed closeness when the couple can devote their energies exclusively to each other or to interests which they jointly or individually develop. Working wives may replace their commitment to the children to some extent by increased interest in their work and this may bring new stimulus into the marriage. The wife may appear to her husband in a new light. He may take pride in her achievements although he may find it difficult to accept her success in the outside world which he was used to regarding as his exclusive sphere, as well as to adjust to the inevitable changes in the division of roles in the house. In a fundamentally sound relationship, the partners manage not to let destructive competition affect their careers and interfere with the marriage. And they may justifiably feel that their new freedom offers possibilities and goals to look forward to, a new life to which their now adult children, and perhaps grandchildren, can add enrichment.

Where a marriage has been kept going 'for the sake of the children' and there is an implicit agreement between the couple to part, once the children have left home, they may in fact discover at that point, that they also stayed together because they have needs of each other. These needs may include hurting, and being uncomfortable with each other. At this time the couple may talk over their problems and decide to stay together. Quite often this arrangement results in an apparent improvement on the surface, with the couple insisting that things are all right between them. Yet an outsider can see that the improvement in the marriage has led to an impoverishment of the personalities of both partners.

For childless couples the midlife crisis may be less clearly defined and while the symptoms may be the same, the implications may differ. The wife has probably always had a job and the change in the family situation may not be so evident. On the other hand, the wife's menopause may precipitate a depression about the absence of offspring. The prospect of getting old without children and grandchildren and without a feeling of family continuity may increase both partners' doubts about the value of their lives. Couples whose children leave home have to change their pattern of living and this, however difficult, may itself provide a challenge and make for fresh impetus. This is less obvious in the midlife of childless couples. For them there may not be a decisive point at which the need for change becomes apparent, but this need will become especially strong in marriages in which there is a great age difference between partners. Whether it is the wife who feels that she has lost her youthfulness and confidence after the menopause, or the husband who seems to be ageing faster than his wife and is afraid to lose her, the couple need to find a new adjustment. Special problems may arise, if the wife was her husband's student, assistant, secretary or in any other role where she looked up to him. As time went on, she may have gained further qualifications, increasing her status. The husband may now find himself to be the weaker partner and have difficulties adjusting to the changed roles.

In satisfactory childless marriages, couples may seek major changes in their lives, in an unconscious attempt to counteract the strain and threatening flatness of the midlife crisis. They may move house, change jobs, follow new hobbies or activities or develop a sudden passion for travel. This may sound like escapism, but it may also lead to development and adjustment in preparation for inevitable changes in the future.

Our question when looking at the midlife crisis, as when looking at any other crisis, must be—what has been highlighted by this crisis, both in the relationship between the couple and in the relationship patterns of each partner? When the midlife crisis presents with insurmountable stress, it is important to understand whether the cause lies in the couple's difficulty in adjusting to the new situation, as in the cases of the Turners and the Shepherds; and, if so, if it can be used to mobilize the couple's potential for development, or whether the crisis highlights chronic problems both in the marriage and in the individuals concerned.

The example of the *Smith family* shows particularly clearly how unresolved conflicts stemming from earlier phases of development may be stirred up at each subsequent stage involving change in the family situation.

When we met the Smith family they had been married for eighteen years and had two teenage sons and a daughter aged eight. The presenting problem was the husband's affair with his secretary and his wife's hysterical response to it. Mrs Smith agreed with her husband that she behaved irrationally, and thus provoked the rejection which she so desperately feared. Mr Smith presented himself as a man whose life was regulated by logic and reason; to this he owed his achievements—he was in an executive job.

During counselling it emerged that Mrs Smith had been an only child whose father had always been ill, suffering from asthma with severe choking attacks. He was hardly ever able to work and her mother not only earned the family's living but was also the perfect housewife. She was worshipped by the sick father and idealized by her daughter. The only critical remark which Mrs Smith allowed herself was that her mother was not always patient enough with the suffering father. She herself understood him much better and indeed often undertook to care for him and spent much time with him alone. She repeatedly stressed how different she was from her mother as she was shy and ineffective, always insisting, 'I can never be like my mother.' It seems likely that she remained so weak and childlike for fear of becoming a rival to her mother. Although she insisted on describing her family as loving and mutually supportive, she revealed to her caseworker childhood nightmares in which she had dreamed that her parents had put a serpent into her bed to get rid of her. Now she found herself preoccupied with sexual fantasies which her husband often provoked by boasting of the sexual satisfaction which his mistress gave him. In his marriage he had not always been potent without stimulation by his wife. Although he presented the picture of a man who was always in control of himself and his life, he was fundamentally insecure in relation to women. He had felt himself dominated by a powerful mother, and one motive for choosing his wife was that she appeared to be the opposite of her, weak, submissive and dependent. His father, like his wife's, had been weak and damaged and the couple shared the image of destroyed fathers and powerful mothers, and were determined to avoid a repetition of this pattern in their own marriage, in which they asserted the opposite: the husband had to be strong and dominant, and the wife helpless and dependent. In this way they perpetuated the defences built up in childhood when Mrs Smith kept herself weak for fear of destroying her loving family and becoming a rival to her mother, and Mr Smith denied all feeling for fear of suffering his father's fate and becoming dominated by women.

The couple's joint flight into an extreme opposite of the pattern of their parents' marriage was, however, only partially appropriate to the needs of their personalities and resulted in considerable strain. There were frequent rows and the marriage was often near breaking point.

In the course of counselling Mrs Smith gained in strength and independence. She also became aware that her sons and her husband, far from feeling threatened by her growing strength, felt supported by it. Mr Smith began to realize the great strain which he had imposed on himself by denying all emotions and became able to be a more relaxed man. When the contact with the couple was terminated after ten months' work, both partners had understood that the recent crisis was a symptom of their unresolved anxieties about their situation in their childhood families. This new awareness was not only a new bond between them, it also made it possible for them to relate more realistically to each other, as well as to their children and their parents.

When fourteen years later the family got in touch with us the marriage had worked extremely well up to the last three years. The husband had set up a business of his own in which his wife's newly developed self-confidence had been of tremendous help. When the children grew up and their careers took them away from home, the couple were very happy in their renewed two person relationship, until a point three years ago when several things had happened. First, the wife's mother died, and the loss stirred up some of her childhood anxieties and feelings of guilt. At that time, too, Mrs Smith went through her menopause, put on weight and felt herself to be unattractive and increasingly uninterested in sex. The eldest son married an exceptionally attractive girl, somebody with whom Mrs Smith felt she could never compete. The second son, who had always been closest to her, continued to live at home. He had several serious girlfriends to whom his mother showed warm hospitality, as long as there was no threat of marriage. Recently, however, he had become seriously involved with an older and very intelligent girl, and his mother was torn between her wish to see them happy and her wish not to lose her son to her. The sexual excitement around the house was disturbing to Mrs Smith because it highlighted her own lack of sexual interest and also because it obviously stimulated her husband's sexuality.

The fact that the daughter now worked in her father's business in close association with him, created additional anxieties. She had developed into an outstandingly attractive girl, and after several years of exciting work abroad, had returned home three years before, just at the time her grandmother died. The way Mrs Smith expressed her admiration for her daughter and her anxious denial of rivalry between them was reminiscent of her earlier attitude to her mother.

Until quite recently Mrs Smith had felt sufficiently valued to be able 'to hold her own', as she put it. Now, however, the husband had appointed a full-time accountant to take over the work which she had been doing so far. Although she herself had felt that this job and the expanding business, in addition to running the house, had been too exhausting, she now felt rejected and angry. She recognized that she behaved in ways similar to those she had used fourteen years ago, and that her husband responded now as then, with provocative behaviour and increased rejection.

Their example strikingly illustrates the principles underlying the 'secret contract' in marriage. There is the unconscious motivation; the compulsive repetition, especially at times of crisis; and the persistence of oedipal feelings.

The couple discovered that in spite of all the changes in their family, their childhood fears of being rejected or dominated by their parents were still so powerful that they had responded to the present stress in much the same way as they had done fourteen years ago. This was a first step towards a joint effort for fresh assessment. Their ability to get through the previous crisis and to recall that experience in the present one, showed their capacity to work on their problems. They could again make use of the therapeutic experience to do so.

The majority of people overcome midlife difficulties without therapeutic help. If help is needed, therapy is really in the last instance about helping people to find their own solutions.

The midlife crisis, it seems, is a particularly propitious time for many couples to find a new and satisfactory solution just because the need to meet it successfully is so great. The sexuality and marriage of the growing children, often coinciding with the death of parents, may strongly reactivate a middle-aged couple's 'oedipal' anxieties. The often traumatic changes in the three generation set-up create a deep need for them to find new meaning in their lives.

A great deal of psychological disturbance can occur in midlife, ranging from serious mental illness to mild anxieties and depression. The reasons for these disturbances can be manifold, and are not always clear. They are by no means all connected with oedipal revivals, but the oedipal theme is the focus of this book and our choice of case-examples shows the reactivation of those feelings. What makes the midlife crisis different from all other crises is that the concern with death as a feature of living is now moving into the centre of the picture, and the screen on to which the old oedipal figures are being cast, is changed once again.

8. Loss, separation and death

Time present and time past
Are both perhaps present in time future,
And time future contained in time past.

> T. S. Eliot, 'Burnt Norton', *Four Quartets*.

Originally we planned to have this quotation at the beginning of
this book, but, now that we are approaching the end of our account
of the life-cycle the quotation seems more appropriate. The reader
has shared with us the experience that each phase of our emotional
life is largely shaped by the previous one and will, inevitably,
affect the next.[60]

Throughout the life cycle, growth involves loss, but loss can also
bring gain. The baby has to leave the security of the mother's womb
to gain life; the growing child begins to find his own identity by
testing out his ability to separate himself from the closeness to his
parents. The adolescent, in making the wrench from life with his
family suffers the pain of separation. Throughout life, at each
phase of change, some familiar position or role has to be given up
so that another can develop. Loss and renewal occur at every stage
from birth to death, and even the finality of death can lead to
renewal for those who have mourned. 'He who has the capacity
to endure guilt and pain, emerges from darkness into dawn and
becomes the survivor, the prospective carrier of life and hope.'[61]
On completing the mourning for what he has lost, the survivor can
welcome a new phase of life as a fresh challenge to psychic growth,
in spite of the pain of loss. Even death can then be 'the final stage
to growth'.[62]

Guilt and pain are inseparable from loss; secrets in the family
are often an attempt to avoid guilt and the pain of loss. The need
to maintain such secret systems can create inflexibility and prevent
adaptation to the multiple challenges and changes of family life.
Secrets between family members are likely to inhibit trusting
relationships and are therefore destructive.

The very different families we have described all show that the greatest need of human beings, from the first to the last breath, is to make and maintain significant personal relationships. The ability to relate is the key to life and to growth.

We want to show how differently people can respond to loss, separation and death.

Mr Woods asked for an opportunity to talk after he had watched a television programme on bereavement. He was in his early thirties and had been married for seven years when his wife died, quite suddenly, without any warning, leaving him with a three-month-old baby daughter, their first child. Naturally he was at first completely shattered, but determined not to part with the baby. His sister, who lived near and was pregnant herself, gave up her job immediately to look after *Sonja* during the day, while her father went to work. Mr Woods felt that having his baby to care for was the greatest help in coping with his grief. When we met him, ten months after his wife's death, he said that he was just beginning to acknowledge that his terrible loss could also have an element of gain. Without it he would never have had the close relationship with his baby daughter which he had now. Also, just because his fate was somehow exceptional, it had roused a great deal of concern among his contemporaries and he felt it was his task to help others with anxieties about loss. His main question to us was: 'What shall I tell my little girl? And when? Also, should I attempt to remarry soon so that Sonja does not become too dependent on me, and unable to make a relationship with a new mother? If I make her own mother very alive for her, will that interfere with a new relationship?'

Mr Woods then spoke about a friend of his whose father had died when he was a baby. His mother remarried within a year and he had a very good stepfather. About his own father he knew nothing and did not seem to miss him until he became an adolescent. Then, in trying to find his own identity, he became depressed and confused. He felt he would never be able to separate from a father he did not know, because he also would never know how much of himself was like his father. Mr Woods said he wanted to help his daughter not to have such an adolescent problem. How could he give her a true image of her mother, let her mourn her dead mother, without blocking a relationship with a potential stepmother?

We showed Mr Woods our appreciation of his concern and his awareness of the need to be honest with his little girl, and not

secretive about her mother's death. He replied that that awareness
and concern was one of the gains and quoted from *The Dissolution*
by John Donne:

> This (which I am amazed that I can speake)
> This death has with my store
> My use increased.

Surviving a beloved person can become, at least for some, a time
of growth, of becoming more fully human. The way down is also
the way up. 'The survivor . . . may come to incorporate some of
the qualities of the deceased into his own being and from there go
on to discover some new values for himself.'[63]

Mr and Mrs Lake, who met and married in Germany about fifty
years ago, were nearly eighty when we met them. Mr Lake's parents
were wealthy Jews and Mrs Lake's family were cultured but far
from wealthy Christians. Both sets of parents had strongly opposed
the marriage. For the young people who were deeply attached to
their families (especially Mrs Lake) this was most distressing, but
after two trial separations they married secretly, against their
parents' wishes. Within a year both families were faced with severe
difficulties: one through serious illness, the other through a threat
of bankruptcy. In the face of these emergencies the young couple
forgot all the hostility and humiliation and jointly, generously and
efficiently offered their help. This broke down the resistence of
both families and set a pattern for future relationships. The young
couple became the greatly appreciated supporters of their parents
and siblings.

When Hitler came to power, the Jewish husband had to leave
Germany and his non-Jewish wife (in contrast to many partners in
similar situations) joined him without hesitation, although it was
most painful for her to leave her family. In England the husband's
qualifications were useless, and the couple suffered real hardship,
especially when their first child was born. The wife had a long and
difficult confinement during which her strength seemed to give
out. For her husband the event of this birth was the most traumatic
experience of his life. He had been convinced that he would lose
his wife, and it became impossible for him to resume a physical
relationship. He suffered deeply, and so did his wife, a born mother
who would have loved to have lots of children. But, although this

was a marriage of exceptional closeness and trust, the trauma was never talked about; it remained a shared secret never put into words.

Mrs Lake compensated for her disappointment at having only one child, by taking into the house babies whose mothers were unable to look after them. While initially and consciously this arose from the need to help with the family finances, it became a source of great satisfaction to the whole family. The Lakes cherished the big family which they had gained in spite of the 'trauma'.

Meanwhile the husband had compensated for the loss of his profession by acquiring a new career, in which he became outstandingly successful. When their only daughter married they warmly welcomed her husband and their three children, who were devoted to their grandparents and they to them. The foster-children and their families provided a big extended family, and all seemed set for a happy old age. But then the husband, in the course of a minor operation, unexpectedly had not only to have one leg amputated above the knee, but suffered a severe heart-attack after the operation.

It is not only death which precipitates feelings of bereavement. Those who have studied the psychological reactions to the amputation of a limb, which involves the loss of function of a vital part, describe it as grief and depression which can well be compared with the emotion of mourning at the death of a loved one. (Parkes.[64])

Mr Lake's wife, daughter and friends understood and accepted his need for understanding and loving support. His wife nursed him devotedly back into life, and he depended on her like a small child on his mother. To have her as his mother had always been his great (unconscious) need, but when a few years later she developed serious heart trouble, and caused justifiable anxiety, he discovered that he had more strength than he had thought. Looking after his wife then helped him to regain a degree of independence, and gave him great satisfaction.

Now, seven years after the amputation, both Mr and Mrs Lake are what one calls invalids, but their lively interests in particular in the arts, soon make one forget this. Their great love of their daughter and the grandchildren, as well as their foster-children's families, their affectionate concern for their friends, their special gift for hospitality, have made this delicate and often suffering couple a source of attraction and stimulation for all who know them.

They owe this considerable achievement to their ability throughout life to find some gain in their losses.

When talking about secrets in this book, we emphasize the way in which they can restrict relationships and can result in destructive behaviour—an expression of the pent-up guilt which is often connected with secrets. However, as we have seen in the example of Mr and Mrs Lake, secrets can be protective if they are based on love and trust. Mrs Lake's loving readiness to respond to her husband's unconscious call to allow him to be her child was what enabled her to help him when he needed it most.

The story of *Mr Gate* shows what can happen if loss remains separated from the reality of life. Mr Gate was forty-five years old when he was admitted to a psychiatric ward after a suicide attempt which almost succeeded. When he found himself alive, he became deeply depressed and refused any co-operation towards recovery. Treatment with drugs had no effect, but his will to live slowly returned when a psychotherapist helped him to talk. Reluctantly and painfully his story unfolded.

His beloved daughter Yvonne had died sixteen years before at the age of two. His wife and he mourned her deeply and unitedly, but when she was pregnant again, she turned towards life and the future while he felt abandoned in his grief. This became still more painful after the birth of a baby, followed by a second son three years later. The pregnancies and the babies preoccupied the wife, and he began to feel that he had lost her too. In his rivalry with the baby boys, the dead daughter became his own special baby whom he needed to keep alive, and by doing so, was unable to give her up. In his fantasies she kissed him 'Good Morning' when he woke, and 'Good Night' when he went to sleep. He had always liked solitary walks, but now Yvonne became his walking companion. His life with Yvonne took on increasing importance, while his life with his family became more and more meaningless, and he became insurmountably estranged from them.

Meanwhile Yvonne, or rather her ghost, had developed in her father's fantasies into a lovely young girl, and when she would have been fifteen years old, he felt so desperately torn between her and his wife that he made a suicide attempt, which failed. His wife, worried about the intensity of his grief and withdrawal, tried hard to achieve some understanding between them, and made him talk to her about Yvonne. But the more he talked, the more 'odd' he appeared to her. Up to that point his job as a successful engineer had provided some link with reality, but, after the suicide attempt, he felt he could not go on with the job, gave it up and began to work as a funeral director. He felt that Yvonne approved of this job, which brought him nearer to her but his wife was angry that he had thrown away a good job and a pension for this morbid occupation. The estrangement between them grew.

Life became more and more unbearable for Mr Gate. Yvonne was now eighteen years old and a beautiful young woman. He could no longer bear to be separated from her, and made his last suicide attempt.

To tell his story to his psychotherapist and feel understood by him helped Mr Gate to try to find a bridge back to his family and the reality of his life. On his first follow-up visit after his discharge from hospital, he reported that things were much better between him and his wife, and his sons too seemed to welcome him back home. He felt the family could make a new start.

The death of a child during the oedipal phase, or of such a child's parent, (see Mr Green, Chapter 4), greatly endangers the resolution of this phase. There is then no opportunity for testing out the fantasies against a background of reality, and the development which eventually involves renunciation becomes impaired.

If Mr Gates's Yvonne had lived, she might not have been as beautiful and irresistible as she was in his fantasies, and in any case she would not have been exclusively his own. By keeping her alive, he avoided mourning her, could not internalize his loss, and therefore was unable to give her up. The same is true of Mr Green, who lost his mother before he was two, and who transferred her idealized image later in an incestuous relationship on to his daughter. In order to find their way back to reality and their living families, both men had to suffer the pain of loss and the renunciation of the idealized lost person.

A recent publication[65] on overt incest as a family defence against loss confirms our experience that there is a strong link between incest fantasies and loss through death. Material illustrating this link has been frequently brought to our attention, especially through the responses of adult sons and daughters to the loss of a parent.[66]

In spite of a considerable lifting of the taboo on death in the last few years, there is still a tendency 'to protect the children' by hiding from them anything connected with death. Secrecy is maintained at great emotional cost, not because it is realistically helpful to anyone, but because everyone is terrified of the assumed consequences of not maintaining it. The story of Sally is an example:

Sally was five when her brother *Barry*, two years younger, was dying of leukemia. Although she accompanied her parents on their hospital visits to the dying child, nobody ever talked to her about Barry's serious illness and his approaching death. On one of these visits six weeks before Barry's death, the usually playful bright and friendly Sally suddenly started kicking, screaming, biting and cursing the ward doctor who arranged for a child psychiatrist to see her. The psychiatrist who later met Sally and her parents told her story:[67]

After we all played together briefly, Sally alone accompanied me to the playroom. She quickly became engrossed in playing with a family of dolls, who after some minutes, were named after the members of her own family. Initially, Sally had the dolls do neutral, pleasant things together, such as having breakfast or going shopping. Within the next half hour the Barry doll was sent to hospital and the Sally, Mummy and Daddy dolls visited him. Barry doll went back and forth a few times between 'home' and 'hospital', and then Sally announced, 'Now he's going to die.' She abruptly stopped playing and, looking at me with great anxiety, said, 'I mean the Barry doll.' A few minutes later she said that she had two secrets. 'I'll tell you the good secret first. Before I came today, I hadn't seen Barry for a couple of weeks and I thought he was dead already. I'm glad that was a wrong secret.' I agreed that it was good that it was a wrong secret, but wondered what her not-good secret was like. Very quickly looking away, Sally said, 'Barry is going to die, but it has to be a secret. It's got to be a secret because if mummies hear secrets that make them too sad, they get sick and they can't be mummies any more.'

Sally asked me to talk to her parents and afterwards her mother told Sally that she and Daddy knew her secret and wanted to talk about it. Over the next weeks, before and after Barry's death, Sally with obvious relief, raised a number of very important questions. These, age-appropriately, included, 'How will Barry get up to Heaven? Will he eat there? Will he get cold? Will he still have pain in his legs?' She was clearly satisfied with her mother's answers, or, perhaps more correctly, she was satisfied that it was now safe to ask the questions. No longer isolated in her frightening fantasies, she soon proceeded from concrete questions about death to even more significant issues of guilt and retribution: 'Sometimes I got mad if Barry took my doll. Whose fault is it that Barry got sick? Why will Barry die? Did someone make a mistake? Barry is a good boy and he got leukemia. Will I get leukemia?' Her mother commented, 'It's good to feel so close to Sally again. I hadn't noticed how stiff and quiet she'd been looking for such a long time.' To be able to talk freely with her mother helped Sally with her worries, and helped her mother to understand her child.

Sally's ability to develop despite the tragedy in her family required that she should be able to find out the connection between the reality of her brother's fatal illness and her fantasies about the nature of his illness and of death. The sharing of secrets helps this testing out process, in that family members can be freed from the burden of their own fantasies, the phantoms of the mind.

More generally, to be taken into the parents' confidence and share with them a family secret which is to be kept secret from some of the outside world, can become a source of strength and growth to the child.

Whether or not to tell a dying patient about his terminal illness is being hotly debated between those who are terrified of what the truth will do to the patient and his relatives, and those who have experienced the peace and acceptance which may result once the patient knows the truth and can talk about it. There is also relief if the family is not involved in a conspiracy of silence and unhappy deceit.

The effect of facing the truth is often quite striking. *Mrs Lane*, in her middle fifties, suffered from an inoperable cancer, but both her loving husband and her exceptionally caring family doctor pretended that there was nothing seriously wrong and that she would soon feel better. She got more and more difficult and irritable with them both, and complained bitterly to her friends about their stupidity and lack of concern for her. One day, the doctor, sensing the cause of her hostility, made it possible for her to ask: 'Am I going to die?' and when he answered in the affirmative she went on to ask all the many questions she had wanted to ask for many weeks. They talked calmly about her illness, and the time she might have left, and about euthanasia which she dismissed once she felt reassured of being understood and supported.

From that moment the patient's attitude both towards her husband and towards her doctor changed completely. An agnostic, she faced her illness cheerfully and courageously, and remained a conscious and caring human being up to her last minute.

Mrs Heath received a letter from her father's family doctor telling her that her father was suffering from cancer of the lung and had a short life-expectancy. The doctor informed her since she was the eldest child and also a social worker, but insisted that she must keep this information secret. Mrs Heath refused to accept the condition. She felt that in the face of approaching death the family should be united and not be split by secrets. Also she was convinced that her father knew about his fatal illness and wanted to talk about it.

Sure enough, on the first occasion when Mrs Heath was alone with her father, whose confidante she had always been, he said: 'Betty, when I die, you will have to make all the arrangements, and that won't be easy for you, because your mother and your brothers will oppose them.' Without hesitation Betty inquired what her father, who was a retired postman but still active as a local councillor, wanted her to do. To her utter surprise, her father's wish was to have a Roman Catholic funeral. The family, although Church of England on paper, did not belong to any church, but Mrs Heath recalled that her father had spent the first four years of his life under the influence of his Catholic grandmother, a very strong personality and a much loved granny. Recently, in his capacity as a councillor, he had had some connection with a convent school and had become friendly with two of the nuns there, especially with a very elderly one who had reminded him of his grandmother, and of his Catholic childhood. He had told nobody about this (for him) very important secret, but was delighted to be able to share it now with his daughter, who arranged to invite the nuns to the house so that she and the rest of the family could get to know them too. Her brothers, being freemasons, were quite upset by their father's unexpected wish; and the mother (partner in what had been a long and good marriage) commented: 'Your father has always been an awkward chap, and he has to be awkward to the end.'

But the father's obvious relief that he need no longer hide his knowledge about his impending death, and could share with the family his secret about his return to his childhood religion, superseded all doubts and misapprehensions. Up to this moment he had refused to relax and had forced himself with tremendous effort to keep active. After the nuns' first visit in a harmonious family atmosphere, he went to bed and, surrounded by his family and the two nuns, died peacefully and smiling two days later.

His daughter was fully aware how different this death might have been, if she had not resisted the doctor's request for secrecy. As it was, she and her brothers felt that nobody who had witnessed their father's dying could ever be afraid of death. When asked whether she could understand her father's return to religion in the face of death, she said: 'I wonder whether it was a return to his childhood religion, or rather to his earliest love, his grandmother.'

We were struck by the perceptiveness of Mrs Heath's comment, which takes dying back to the beginning, and thus completes the cycle of life. The thoughts and feelings of many dying people centre upon their earliest childhood and on their mothers. For Mr Heath, the person who made him feel safe and held him was his grandmother. She helped him long ago to gain the confidence that made him able to let go, because she had no need to hold him back. People who in their childhood have been discouraged from being separate, and thus gain a separate identity, have difficulties in letting go; they cling. Faced with death they are likely to cling to life, for to die is to accept the last separation, the breaking through the last boundary to the unknown.

The experience of being securely held in earliest childhood, which gives the confidence to let go, will be put to the test again and again, especially in periods of change and risk and perhaps most vividly in sexual love; for when the sexual encounter is complete, it is essentially an experience of letting go and of trust.[68] We can therefore say, that to learn to die is the continuation of learning to live and to love. He who has no fear of life and can relate in love is much more likely to let go of life with acceptance and confidence.

Notes

PROLOGUE

1 The idea of the life cycle is an extremely widespread and ancient one. It is embodied in religion, mythology and legend but as a way of understanding individual development we are most in debt to Erik Erikson whose work we quote directly in other chapters.
E. H. Erikson, *Identity and the Life Cycle*, International Universities Press, New York, 1959.
E. H. Erikson, *Identity: Youth and Crisis*, Faber & Faber, London, 1968.
The application of the idea of a cycle to the life of families has not been so fully worked out in our psychological literature. We have found the short article by A. M. Solomon helpful:
A. M. Solomon, 'A developmental, conceptual premise for family therapy', *Family Process*, **12**, 179–88, 1973.

2 The importance of the influence of secrets in the life of families, especially those sorts of secrets which family members know but realize that they are supposed not to know really, is well known amongst clinicians but has not been much talked of. One of us (C.D.) presented a paper at the Institute of Psychiatry in London in October 1974 entitled 'Open and closed secrets in the family' in which we pointed out that children coming to a child psychiatrist with difficulties could sometimes be helped by getting the family to talk of certain sorts of secrets. At that time we found that two London analysts, quite separately had discovered that children could sometimes be helped through the revelations of family secrets.
A. Bonnard, 'Truancy and pilfering associated with bereavement', *Adolescents: Psychoanalytic Approach to Problem and Therapy*, ed. S. Lorand and H. I. Schneer, Paul B. Hoeber Inc., New York, 1961.
A. Hayman, 'The analysis of an atypical child', *The Psychoanalytic Study of the Child*, **27**, 476–504, 1973.
Phyllis Greenacre has pointed out that it is possible to see the development of the ability of a child to keep family secrets as denoting advances in the child's appreciation of reality and of the boundaries of fact and fantasy. She also suggests that: 'The basic secrets are those of the origins and the fate of life, implied in the riddle of the sphinx, which Oedipus solved and so was permitted to live.' Our whole book indicates the extent to which we are in agreement with Greenacre.
P. Greenacre, 'Further notes on fetishism', 1960, in *Emotional Growth*, International Universities Press, New York, 1971, vol. I, pp. 190–1.

3 The idea that certain processes in families are akin to those that produce myths within society at large has produced some important contributions to

the understanding of families. Our first quotation is from an (as yet) unpublished paper from the Tavistock Clinic:

J. Byng-Hall, 'Family myths and dramas', 1976, (unpublished).

This author has the following paper in print:

'Family myths used as defence in conjoint family therapy', *British Journal of Medical Psychology*, **46**, 239–50.

Our second quotation is from:

A. J. Ferreira, 'Family myths, the covert rules of the relationship', *Confina Psychiatrica*, **8**, 15–20, 1965.

A. J. Ferreira, 'Family myths and homeostasis', *Archives of General Psychiatry*, **9**, 457–63.

The British psychiatrist R. D. Scott has utilized the concept of family myths to understand some of the features of certain instances of schizophrenic mental breakdown.

R. D. Scott, 'The shadow of the ancestor: a historical factor in the transmission of schizophrenia', *British Journal of Medical Psychology*, **42**, 13–32, 1969.

CHAPTER I

4 The basic work for this chapter was carried out whilst attempting to summarize psychoanalytic ideas on the development of the individual.

C. Dare and J. Sandler, 'The psychoanalytic theory of development', (unpublished), 1974.

C. Dare, 'Psychoanalytic theories', Chapter 11 in M. Rutter and L. Hersov (eds.), *Child Psychiatry: Modern Approaches*, Blackwell, London, 1977.

Psychoanalytic theories of development began with Freud's observations that many adults suffering from hysterical forms of neurotic disorders appeared to have suffered from traumatic sexual seductions during childhood.

S. Freud, 'Studies on Hysteria', *Standard Edition*, **2**, 1895.

At that time, in the 1890s, Freud thought that the young child was unable to cope with the excitation of seduction and the immature mind caused the experience to be stored in such a way as to appear later as symptoms. Later Freud came to believe that what he had before taken to be memories of his patients' resulting from seductions and like sexual experiences were in fact the outcome of intense but forbidden childhood sexual wishes leading them to fantasize sexual experiences. This theory, which was essentially developed in order to understand the origins of adult neuroses, led Freud to consider the course of development of childhood mental life. Subsequently the practice of psychoanalytic treatments included an aim on the part of the analyst to help his patients establish a rather complete and detailed knowledge of their own personal development so as to enable them to understand the sources of their adult personality and its problems as being comprehensibly derived from their earlier mental life. Psychoanalytic theories of development, therefore, are generalizations about the course of childhood as reconstructed during the psychoanalytic treatment of patients, supplemented and modified by direct observations on babies and older children and the treatment observations of older children. Freud's views on the development of sexuality in children are to found in:

S. Freud, 'Three essays on the theory of sexuality', *Standard Edition*, **7**.

The views on development that the authors have are derived from the many psychoanalysts who have made huge additions and amendments to Freud's work in this area.

5 Of the near contemporary psychoanalysts who have had an enormous impact upon the development of understanding of the psychological growth of very little children, Donald Winnicott and Melanie Klein are the most influential. Winnicott is of especial importance to us in this work because of his detailed and inspired understanding of the mother-infant relationship which is the beginning of the three person family.

The quotation is from:

D. W. Winnicott, *The Family and Individual Development*, Tavistock Publications, London, 1965, p. 47.

The New York analyst, Margaret S. Mahler, has worked over many years to understand the early development of children both in the course of clinical treatments and in systematic observation. Her findings are expressed in more traditional psychoanalytic terms than are the works of Donald Winnicott. None the less the work of these two writers are complementary in a very important way for our ability to conceptualize the earliest development of a child's sense of self.

M. S. Mahler, F. Pine and A. Bergman, *The Psychological Birth of the Human Infant*, Hutchinson, London, 1975.

6 It is impossible for us to refer to the major works of these authors. We will simply list the following writings introductory to the ways of thinking that we have absorbed from them.

A. Freud, *Normality and Pathology in Childhood*, Hogarth Press, London, 1966.

S. Freud, *Three Essays on the Theory of Sexuality*, Standard Edition, **7**, 1905.

M. Klein, *The Psycho-Analysis of Children*, Hogarth Press, London, 1932.

M. Balint, *The Basic Fault*, Tavistock Publications, London, 1968.

D. W. Winnicott, *Through Paediatrics to Psycho-Analysis*, Hogarth Press, London, 1975.

7 E. H. Erikson, *Identity and the Life Cycle*, International Universities Press, New York, 1959, pp. 56–7.

8 S. Freud, *The Ego and the Id*, Standard Edition, **19**, 1923.

9 W. R. D. Fairbairn, *Psychoanalytic Studies of the Personality*, Tavistock Publications, London, 1952.

10 M. Klein, *Envy and Gratitude*, Tavistock Publications, London, 1957.

11 M. Balint, *The Basic Fault*, Tavistock Publications, London, 1968.

12 D. W. Winnicott, *The Family and Individual Development*, Tavistock Publications, London, 1965, p. 5.

13 D. W. Winnicott, 'Ego distortion in terms of true and false self', 1960, Chapter 12 in *The Maturational Process and the Facilitating Environment*, Hogarth Press, London, 1972.

14 K. Horney, *Feminine Psychology*, Routledge & Kegan Paul, London, 1967.

15 Melanie Klein's exposition of these views are contained in part in the publications of 1932 and 1957 mentioned above. A monograph of her own that puts forward her understandings with great clarity is:
M. Klein, 'Our adult world and its roots in infancy', 1959, in *The Writings of Melanie Klein*, Hogarth Press, London, 1975, vol. III.

16 J. Rickman, 'The factor of number in individual- and group-dynamics', 1950, in *Selected Contributions to Psycho-Analysis*, Hogarth Press, London, 1957

17 M. Balint, 'On love and hate', 1951, *Primary Love and Psycho-Analytic Technique*, Tavistock Publications, London, 1952.

18 S. Freud, *New Introductory Lectures on Psycho-Analysis, Standard Edition*, **22**, 1933.

19 E. H. Erikson, *Young Man Luther*, Faber & Faber, London, 1958, p. 12.

CHAPTER 2

20 The Institute of Marital Studies, which is part of the Tavistock Institute of Human Relations, and of which the senior author was a founder member, has produced a large number of contributions to the theory and therapy of marriage.
Those most relevant for this chapter are:
Lily Pincus, (ed.), *Marriage: Studies in Emotional Conflict and Growth*, Methuen, London, 1955.
K. Bannister and L. Pincus, *Shared Phantasy in Marital Problems: Therapy in a Four-Person Relationship*, Tavistock Institute of Human Relations, London, 1965.
L. Guthrie and J. Mattinson, *Brief Casework with a Marital Problem*, Tavistock Institute of Human Relations, London, 1971.
An important contribution to the conceptualization of marriage upon which we draw also derives from the Tavistock Clinic:
H. V. Dicks, *Marital Tensions*, Routledge and Kegan Paul, London, 1967.

21 The general principles to which we are referring are those of psycho-analytic psychology. These have been called the basic assumptions of psychoanalysis:
J. Sandler, C. Dare and A. Holder, 'Frames of reference in psychoanalytic psychology. III: A note on the basic assumptions', *British Journal of Medical Psychology*, **45**, 143–7, 1972.

22 There is a problem that arises constantly in psychodynamic psychologies; this is that Freud and many who have followed him used a number of

crucial concepts in ways that changed with time. At one time Freud used the notion of unconsciousness purely descriptively. At other times he used the word unconscious more technically in talking of a hypothetical apparatus of the mind, 'The Unconscious'. One of us has been involved in a prolonged project attempting to elucidate problems in these areas:

J. Sandler, A. Holder and C. Dare, 'Frames of reference in psychoanalytic psychology. VI. The topographical frame of reference: the Unconscious', *British Journal of Medical Psychology*, **46**, 37–43, 1973.

23 A. Freud, *The Ego and the Mechanisms of Defence*, Hogarth Press, London, 1936.

24 R. D. Laing, *The Self and Others*, Tavistock Publications, London, 1961.

25 J-P. Sartre, *Words. Reminiscences of Jean-Paul Sartre*, Hamish Hamilton, London, 1964.

CHAPTER 3

26 The birth of the first baby as the event signalling the appearance of a new two-generation nuclear family has not begun to be investigated until very recently. Indeed we remain sure that far too little is known about the psychological processes surrounding this stupendous event. We are most grateful to the Institute of Marital Studies for allowing us to read and learn from a draft of an extremely thorough and creative review of the literature in this field.

Institute of Marital Studies, '*Marriage and birth of a baby*', Preliminary *Literature Survey*, I.M.S. Serial Number 390.

27 D. W. Winnicott, Primary maternal preoccupation, (1956). In: D. W. Winnicott *Through Paediatrics to Psycho-Analysis*, Hogarth Press, London, 1975.

28 The changing social climate whereby it is increasingly important that women are able to feel as fully absorbed in a career as their husbands is associated with the gradual, and painful, evolution of new styles of marital partnerships. This is most clearly evident in self-consciously liberated women who are usually members of the well educated and middle classes. Interesting studies in this area are now appearing. e.g.:

R. Rapoport and R. N. Rapoport, *Dual-Career Families*, Penguin Books, Harmondsworth, 1971.

29 P. Lomas, 'The husband-wife relationship in cases of puerperal breakdown', *British Journal of Medical Psychology*, **32**, 117–23, 1959.

30 The importance of the widespread depression experienced by mothers living with pre-school children in contemporary urban society, is beginning to be documented although as yet there have been no comparably widespread efforts to help with the problem.

G. W. Brown, M. N. Bhrolchain and T. Harris, 'Social class and psychiatric disturbance among women in an urban population,' *Sociology*, **9**, 225–54, 1975.

31 N. Richman, 'Depression in mothers of pre-school children', *Journal of Child Psychology and Psychiatry*, **17**, 75–6, 1976.

32 See P. Lomas (1959), above.

33 A. Lyons, 'Marriage Problems', (Unpublished manuscript.)

34 K. P. Eissler, *The Psychiatrist and the Dying Patient*, International Universities Press, New York, p. 149, 1955.

CHAPTER 4

35 Freud's first observations on the derivatives of childhood sexuality in his adult patients had led him to believe, as we have said, that young children had sexual desires for their parents, especially the one of the opposite sex. Later he thought of the infant as having even earlier manifestations of sexuality than those which led him to wish to possess his mother (or her her father). These earliest forms of sexuality did not impel the child to seek a relationship with another person for gratification but were of an auto-erotic nature. The observant reader of Freud's *Three Essays on the Theory of Sexuality*, will notice that the footnotes to the *Standard Edition* show that all the references to sexuality in childhood as a phenomenon preceding the oedipal phase were added by Freud after his first edition.
S. Freud, *Three Essays on the Theory of Sexuality*, Standard Edition, **7**, 1905.
In the psychoanalytic literature the difference between derivatives in adult mental life of the oedipal and the pre-oedipal phases, are given considerable importance. In general problems arising from disturbance of the oedipal phase of life are thought to be less likely to give rise to severe difficulties. 'Fixations' derived from the pre-oedipal period are considered likely to be more sinister.

36 The concept of *basic trust* is widely used. Early psychoanalysts placed great emphasis on the relationship between the mouth and early infantile mental life. This view has been studied intensively:
J. Sandler and C. Dare, 'The psychoanalytic concept of orality', *Journal of Psychosomatic Research*, **14**, 211–22, 1970.
Erikson extended the notion that general traits of optimism or pessimism in the adult character derived from the first year experiences of the infant, to the notion of *basic trust* in an extremely influential book:
E. H. Erikson, *Childhood and Society*, Norton, New York, 1946.

37 The fascinating case histories of Freud's early writings, including those he wrote up with his colleague Josef Breuer, exemplify this:
S. Freud and J. Breuer, *Studies on Hysteria*, Standard Edition, **2**.

38 M. Balint, *The Basic Fault*, Tavistock Publications, London, 1968.

39 See Harold F. Searles, 'Oedipal love and the Counter-Transference', *Collected Works*, Hogarth Press, London, 1965.

40 The widespread existence of representations of incest in myths and legends attests to the pervasiveness of the fascination and the horror that the subject of incest evokes in people over the range of history and geography. Freud, of course, drew upon the Greek legend of the fate of Oedipus to characterize what he took to be a universal problem of human development. Levi-Strauss demonstrates that there are close parallels between the legend of Oedipus as described by, for example, Sophocles, and myths of incest amongst the Pueblo tribes:
C. Levi-Strauss, *Structural Anthropology*, Basic Books, New York, 1963.
Among more recent works of literature in which the theme of incest is pursued we want to mention a novel by Thomas Mann, *The Holy Sinner*, Penguin Modern Classics, 1975.
In this story, set in mediaeval Europe, a son born as the result of the incestuous love of a brother and sister, returns unknown to his mother's place, and, falling in love with her as she with him, they repeat the incestuous crime and yet are able to avoid eternal damnation.

41 There are few psychoanalysts, or any other authors for that matter, who have been able to look at the importance of 'normal' development of the potential for incest in a family. The fact that the incestuous wishes of the child are not totally the product of fantasy, but are partially mirrored by real wishes in the parents, enables the child to envisage a future sexual life. Adelaide Johnson, from whom this quotation is taken, was one of the few writers on the subject of incest who seems to have been able to see the maturational aspects of the parental counter-oedipal response. This quotation is from:
D. B. Robinson (ed.), *Experience, Affect and Behavior: Psychoanalytic Explorations of Dr Adelaide McFayden Johnson*, The University Press, Chicago, 1969, pp. 398–9.

42 C. G. Jung, 'Symbols of Transformation', *Collected Works*, vol. V, Routledge & Kegan Paul, London.

43 H. Maisch, *Incest*, Andre Deutsch, London, 1973, p. 147.

44 S. Freud, *Totem and Taboo, Standard Edition*, **13**, p. 125 and p. 17, 1913. Throughout this work Freud relies heavily upon the anthropological studies of J. G. Frazer, especially *Totemism and Exogamy*, 1910.

CHAPTER 5

45 P. Blos, *On Adolescence*, The Free Press, Glencoe, 1962.
As well as providing here an overall survey of adolescence Blos has also described, with great sensitivity, a series of case studies in his book *The Young Adolescent*, Macmillan, New York, 1970.

46 K. Bannister, and L. Pincus, *Shared Phantasy in Marital Problems: Therapy in a Four-Person Relationship*, Tavistock Institute of Human Relations, London, 1965.

CHAPTER 6

47 D. W. Winnicott, 'Adolescence: struggling through the doldrums' (1961), Chapter 10 in his book *The Family and Individual Development*, Tavistock Publications, London, 1961.

48 S. Freud, 'Family romances', A note to *Three essays on Sexuality*, Standard Edition, **9**, 1909.

49 E. H. Erikson, *Identity: Youth and Crisis*, Faber & Faber, London, 1968.

50 E. H. Erikson, *Young Man Luther*, Faber & Faber, London, 1958, p. 12.

51 J. Bowlby, 'Separation: Anxiety and Anger', *Attachment and Loss*, Hogarth Press, London, 1973, vol. 2, pp. 322–3.
This quotation from Dr Bowlby does little to demonstrate the great importance he has had in his role at the Tavistock Clinic, in the formulation not only of attachment theory, but also of family models of understanding the nature of child development.

52 N. W. Ackerman, *The Psychodynamics of Family Life*, Basic Books, New York, 1958, p. 225.

53 E. Buxbaum, *Troubled Children in a Troubled World*, International Universities Press, New York, 1970, p. 261.

54 E. Jacobson, *The Self and the Object World*, International Universities Press, New York, 1964, p. 170.

55 I. Boszormenyi-Nagy and G. M. Spark, *Invisible Loyalties*, Harper & Row, Hagerstown, 1973, p. 107.
The enormous willingness of children to play the part in their parents' lives that served the parents' own ends rather than those of their offspring, is a remarkable clinical phenomenon. Boszormenyi-Nagy's concept of loyalty evokes both the power and the positive love that leads children to fulfil their parents' complex needs and ambitions.

56 T. Parsons, 'The incest taboo in relation to social structure and the socialization of the child', *British Journal of Sociology*, **5**, 101–17, 1954.

57 H. Deutsch, *Selected Problems of Adolescence*, International Universities Press, New York, 1968, pp. 103–4.

58 We have not been able to say much at all about cultural change and cultural differences although we have tried to show that we are aware of the extent to which our observations are bound to be limited by the perspective afforded by our own time and place. Usually, of course, we have

to be sensitive with our patients and clients, to the extent to which the differences in culture, generation and social class add caution to our interpretation. In working with teenagers, these problems are especially crucial. As a model for the understanding of cultural change and its effect on adolescent development, Spiegel's work is of great interest:

J. P. Spiegel, 'The resolution of role conflict within the family', Chapter 30 in: N. W. Bell and E. F. Vogel, (eds.), *A Modern Introduction to the Family*, The Free Press, New York, 1957.

CHAPTER 7

59 Until relatively recently psychoanalytic theory has had very little to say about the time of the life cycle after young adulthood. In part associated with this theoretical lacuna there has been a tendency within clinical practice to suppose that more elderly people are unlikely to receive much help from psychoanalytical psychotherapies. The situation amongst Jungian analysts has been different for both their theory and practice gives some stress to the idea that important phases of the development of the person are encountered in middle age. However both the authors, from their experience of working the one with more elderly couples with marital disturbance, and the other with whole families including parents or grand-parents well past youth, found that useful therapeutic work, including psychological growth and change, could be achieved. Further, a number of psychoanalysts have established interest in midlife and ageing problems. There was a significant paper in this field from the pen of E. Jacques:

'Death and the midlife crisis', *International Journal of Psycho-Analysis*, 1965, **40**, 502–16.

Just recently we have heard of a five-year project underway for about one year at the Sigmund Freud Institute in Frankfurt entitled 'Project Mid-Life' with which is associated the distinguished psychoanalyst, A. Mitscherlich.

J. Marmor, 'The crisis of middle age', *American Journal of Orthopsychiatry*, **37**, 336–7, 1967.

CHAPTER 8

60 The taboos that we observe in our society around the subject of death and mourning seem to us to have a parallel to the taboos around the facts of human relationships that make incest both possible and horrible. In this chapter we have been able to note that sometimes the two themes come together. In our work with individuals, couples and families we find that the themes of reactions and responses to death are as insistent as are the themes of the possibilities and the fears of incest. The major secrets of family life are truly the origins and fate of life.

Bowlby initiated interest in loss as a research topic at the Tavistock Clinic:

J. Bowlby, 'Grief and mourning in infancy and early childhood', *Psycho-analytic Study of the Child*, **15**, 9–52, 1960.

However the interest in the psychological importance of experiences of loss dates from Freud's paper: 'Mourning and melancholia', *Standard Edition*, **14**, 243–58.

Melanie Klein put especial emphasis on the fear of loss, especially the infant's fear of the loss of his mother as result of his own angry and destructive wishes towards his loved ones:

M. Klein, 'Mourning and its relation to manic-depressive states,' 1940, Chapter 20, in: *The Writings of Melanie Klein*, vol. I, Hogarth Press, London, 1975.

Further work at the Tavistock Institute of Human Relations includes that by Colin Murray Parkes. See Note 64 below.

61 E. Seligman, 'On death and survival', *The Analytical Psychology Club*, **22**, 135, 1976.

62 E. Kubler-Ross, *Death: The Final Stage of Growth*, Prentice-Hall, New Jersey, 1975.

63 E. Seligman. The quotation is from her paper referred to in Note 61.

64 C. M. Parkes, *Bereavement: Studies of Grief in Adult Life*, Tavistock Publications, London, 1975, p. 184.

65 Thomas G. Guthell and Nicholas C. Avery, 'Multiple incest as a family defence against loss', *Family Process*, New York, 1977.

66 Lily Pincus, *Death and the Family*, Pantheon, New York, 1974, Faber & Faber, London, 1976.

67 Nina S. Evans, 'Mourning and Family Secrets', *Journal of American Academy of Child Psychiatry*, vol. XV, 1976.

68 E. Seligman. We have found the idea to be expressed with great beauty in her paper referred to in Note 61.

Index of Authors

Subject Index

LILY PINCUS. Born in Germany in 1898, she came to England during the Hitler years. She became a social worker in a family casework agency. She is a founder of the Tavistock Institute for Marital Studies. *Death and the Family* (Faber, 1976), one of several books of which she is author or co-author, was written ten years after the death of her husband.

CHRISTOPHER DARE B.A., M.B., B. Chir., M.R.C.P., M.R.C. Psych., D.P.M. Born in Devon in 1937 he studied medical science and psychology at Cambridge and qualified as a doctor at Guy's Hospital. He is an associate member of the British Psychoanalytical Society, and trained as a child psychiatrist at the Tavistock Clinic. He is now a consultant psychiatrist at the Maudsley Hospital.

He lives in South London with his family of five children.